What Is It Press Copy
Editor: Sebastian De
Author: Sue Yan
Series Start Date: 11-20-2013
Revised: 03-28-2020
ISBN: 978-0-9679947-7-2
ASIN: B07GCWL17L
GGKEY: LCFQCNPLU0R

The manual (SM069) is no longer provided in the appendix of the books in the Empty Nation (EN) series because it grew beyond a reasonable size. So it's published separately on Amazon (small cost), Google Play Books (free) and also available for free when you purchase this title on Audible.com, the accompanying PDF support material (SM069) will be available in your Audible Library along with the audio book.

References to Manual are made throughout the books in the series. Tag format: the word being referenced is tagged in **bold** print preceding the reference in square brackets. Reference format: a period [.] the dot symbol is used to separate the components of the reference, as in the following examples.

Tag [*section* dot *sub-section* dot *description*]

SIT [4.D-G2.22], section 4, sub-section D-G2, description 22
PBS [2.10], section 2, description 10
SEC [26], section 26

EN04: Careers

C01 College Part C: Gurls attend a lecture on, whitey domination and Caucasian penis insecurities. And about why the American Vaganus® is our new gold. Off to Washingcum DC to start careers in politics. Rimme announces Mary's appointed to run the Poop program to save poor American orphaned babies. The Orphans are actually farm breed Homo-Sis-Sapiens created to infiltrate the world and to gain sexual & financially hegemony through Vaganus® addiction.

C02 Off We Go: Poop Cum-firmation, Yanket probes Mary hard about Sissydom loyalty. The Nunnery comforts the Gurls with an orgy. Then they meet Cardinal Jackeroff and she administers Holy Cum-Union then inserts her penance. Cardinal Jackeroff discusses HCC Sissy Nuns in politics.

C03 POOP: Mr. Jamitin Bootee the African Union envoy makes a deal for the MSES. Mary swears to uphold the Second Cunt-Stitution. The Gurls deliver the first batch of orphaned Sissy babies. Girl-on-Gurl time with Mrs. Bootee. All the families adopting the Sissy babies are CI. In Africa, the white Sissy child is a trophy of conquest.

C04 Networking: The jungle mission in LA is a joint-venture. The HCC & USA Inc. attempt to dominate the world. As usual the Gurls are unharmed but their HCC Nun Mothers get into a pre-dick-ament which they help them out of.

C05 Back in DC: Mary suggests using weapons of massive Poopalation. Mary exposes Russian intervention. HCC training doctors to installing MSES devices. Bombshell on Moms, Jane and I are knocking you guys up!

C06 Eurasia: Russia, India make a deal with Mary the diploma to install PDE-SSAAAS devices. The Gurls do a fuckfest experiment for their visa. If an employer cooperates with the MSES they get free Sissy booty for life!

C07 Mommy Time: Mary & Jane plan wedding stuff. Marriage ceremony for Mary & Sandy, Jane & Heather. The Gurls knock-up each other's Mom! Gurl say bye to their Mom-wives.

C08 Capitol Hill: Mary plays with Popoff and gets a ticket from the LCT Violations Bureau. Roasted NS Man-Sausage is rated the best American specialty dish of the year in 2253. Back in the office, Mary fields calls, Bootie, the Farm and Pooty. Mary is successful at creating a beachhead for MSES in India, Africa and Latin America & Russia.

Books in the Empty Nation (EN) Series

Empty Nation

A dirty story about a dirty country

Series (1), Book (4)

Careers

Sue Yan Nish

Table of Contents

Chapter 1: College Part C

The year is 2254...

[1.1] FUCIT

Senior year at FUCIT...

Chop, chop.... let's go Honey Bunny!

Geeez... What's your rush Cum-mandant Mary? Ahh... Can we pleeeease... just sleep in and finish college too? Kiss... Cum back to bed I wanna play some more. Mwah...

Yep! After we graduate, you can play and sleep in all you want, let's go! You little adorable Fuck-Monkey®. Mwah... I love you, cum-on!

Ugh! God-of-Cocks it's too early to learn anything!

Cum on, cum on, this is the last year Jane let's get it over with!

The Gurls got up & dressed...

Yep! I'm with you. In body only, my mind is still thinking about last night's party. Uooogh! Ahhh... You look so good babe! The power-suite turns me on. Kisss... Ahhh... I'll be your little Bitch forever. Mwah... Mwah...

You too Gurl! Mwah... I like the stockings, garter-belt skirtini combination, really nice, very sassy looking. But seriously, I'm just glad you don't prance around naked anymore. Kiss...

Hmmm... You're my grown-up little Gurl® now! Kiss... See what four years of college can do for you!

Yes Mommy... Haahaa... (Jane does a pouty face).

Okay, out the door! We gotta get to class. We'll talk on the way... Cum on! Move, move, move...

Ooooh... I love the Federal University of Cultural Integration Transition, the **FUCIT** [3.C1.4] campus, just breathing in the fresh air... Ahhh!

Yep! The trees, the flowers, the ivy growing on the brick walls of the lecture halls.

Yeah, The scholarly feeling of academia just makes me wanna squirt. Oooh! Shoot! I'm lactating. Ahh... Yeah there you go Honey, suckle on Mommy while we walk. Oooh... Up you go! (Jane jumped up into Mary's arms). Yeah suck on my tit you hungry child. Ummm.... Wow Jane you're still so light, it's like carrying a baby. Agh! (Jane being a B-Type Gurl is tiny compared to Mary).

Ummm... Oh that feels sooo good, thanks Baby. I love this place! FUCIT is so wonderful. I can study here the rest of my life.

Yeah, I feel the same way. Everything about it and the career moves the Archbishop and Cardinal are talking to us about.

Yep! They've been planning our course loads since freshmen year. And Jane, you know they're grooming us for political careers it's obvious. So it's only gonna get better from here Honey. All the money is in politics and banking.

Heee hee… Yeah, I can smell the sweet fragrance of the money we're gonna be making from the cool government jobs we'll have after graduation. Ahhh... Here we are Long Dong hall.

Jizz-Us® [9.I3.0] Look at all the students in the lecture hall. Holy-Cock! There's gotta be over two hundred students here.

Wow! Cum on Jane let's sit in the front (Mary being the DOM always takes the lead and drags Jane by the hand into the lecture hall).

Ooooh! This feels good, I like how the seat probes are warn. It just feels so much nicer when you wiggle your pussy down onto them, hmmm! And you know me? I love a nice long dong up my cooch during a lecture. Haaa haa... And the hall is appropriately named.

Yeah Mare I like the seat-probes they have here at college too, pre-warned & lubed. Way better than the cold, dry one's we had back in high school. And these probes even vibrate. So what's this class about? (Mary of course handles all the class registrations and assignments for both of them).

This course is about government and its mandatory for the all students taking the US Civil Servant exam.

Right, right… According to Yaoi & Rimme we won't know how to rule the world if we don't educate ourselves about the importance of the **Vaganus**® [14.O1.6] and the role it plays in the American global governance doctrine. Ooooh! I squirted! I gotta turn down the vibration on the probe. It feels sooo good! Ahhh…

[1.2] AGG

American Global Governance (AGG)...

Good morning! I'm Professor **Orgazzie**. You'll be studying how the American doctrine for the domination of the world is applied, legally or not, to other places in the world. Any questions?

Yes? Professor I think I'm in the wrong lecture hall.

Okay. What are you a freshman?

Ahhh... Kinda new here.

And you don't know your way around the campus?

No Sir! I mean, Professor I'm a transfer student from **Hardon-Vard** university.

Oh, oh... Then well cum to FUCIT. Ah... Where do you need to go?

To Piss-on-me Annex.

Oooh! Well just go out from here and turn right, it's the third hall on the left next to the Gory-Hole Monument.

Thanks Professor **Orgazzie**!

Okay! So a lot of you are senior students here to prep for the US Civil Servant exam. And rightfully so. The exam is a no mess around test which many students fail the first time they take it. I don't mean to discourage any of you, but the exam is intense and you'll need to study rigorously.

Wow, Hmmm... (Grumble, grumble from the worried students).

Well, now that I've scared you, judging from the way most of you are squirming on your seat-probes. Let's start by defining the doctrine. Then we'll go into the problems associated with the infiltration of **Sissydom**® into the Sissy-less Cunt-tries or USA Inc. occupied territories like Mexico and Canada.

Now, we know morality plays an important role in this discussion. So it's really a crap-shoot! Haaa haa… I mean, government is a game of chance. As in the previous millenniums people would debate over the righteousness of their religion, moral convictions or the correctness of their government's interventions into other Cunt-tries. Yada, yada, ya… The later refers to Cunt-tries with the Caucasian-White race in it. Who through imperialism, pretty much came ever so close to destroying all of civilization on this planet. I mean, we're really lucky we weren't. Huh! Here I'll quote one of the greatest comedians of all time, Lewis Black,

> *Vaporized in a Nuclear*
> *FIRE-FUCK-BALL…!!!…*

Huuuuh… Oooooh… Whoa! (The students are all gasping in shock of the Professors frightening statement).

Yeah, yeah… Hard to believe, right? Nuclear-Fuck-Holocaust. So, here I have to pause and explain the whole story about how this world would've been better off without the white race. Now I know what you're thinking, how could this white guy be wishing he didn't exist? Well let's first analyze the contribution of the Caucasian-White race to peace in the world.

So in the beginning Whitey was mostly the European's. Then in later years it was the white supremacist enclave of the North

American Cunt-tries, the USA Inc. and our friends to the north, Canada.

But North America in relationship to the destruction of the world is a blurry vision considering the Canadians caved into **Sissydom**® (EN01) almost as quick as a kid does for a candy bar.

Okay I digress. North America is where most of the European Caucasian's went after Europe started be cuming mostly Asian and Middle Eastern. Either though inter-marriage or simply pushed-out by the immigrating hordes after Europe was engulfed into the **Eurasian Union** [23.58.1]. So the last bastion of privileged Caucasian-White race bastards ended up here in North America.

Now that we got that out of the way, let's move on to. Ahhh... what were we talking about?

Whitey Professor!

Oh yeah, Whitey! Well the Caucasian's by fate, inbreeding, genetic mutation, warmongering, chance, greed, by whatever means, had a need to project their insecure selves onto others in the way of conquest. In recent times there have been studies conducted at Peniston, Johns Hopkinky, Hardon-Vard, and here at FUCIT which prove beyond a reasonable doubt, yet unsubstantiated, Caucasian's have smaller penises then all other races in the world. It's that simple.

Huh! What? Ahhh... Are you sure professor? Wow... Oooooh.... Whatta? (The male Stud students are all gasping in shock looking down at their crotch). Hey drink only filtered water! Yeah!

But Professor Orgazzie! Isn't the penis shrinkage caused by the water!

Yes, yes, of course it is, at least this is the rumor. And word has it. The Chinese contaminated the water to end the American Empire. Truth is we were doing a splendid job of destroying ourselves without their help. And don't believe gossip! The Great American Penis Shrinkage, the **GAPS** [23.17] is just a myth! The only ones affected are, the dregs of society, the Non-Stud (NS) workers, living in FEMA camps.

Yep! I know, hard to believe, right? But according to me and some other well-known, depending on who you ask, Sissydom scholars, Whitey has a small dick. This penis-size, inferiority complex, led them to project their fabricated dominance onto others. Not by using their penises mind you! Haa… Haa... that would be kinda silly. No, no, instead to conquer others they used violence and the killing weapons of war.

Hmmm… What is he saying? I'm pretty sure he just accused the White race of genocide. (More mumbling from the young uninformed audience).

Yeah it's hard to believe! Legions of soldiers, monstrously larger ships with bigger swords, spears, canons, battering rams, bigger bombs to project an image of dominance. Bigger stuff to match the superior penis-size of the enemy. And here calling non-Caucasians the enemy is ironic. Because up until the time the European barbarians started their quest to dominate the world, those so-called, enemies, the non-Caucasians, were relatively peaceful civilizations. So okay let's get off this Whitey bashing and continue on the path of why the USA Inc. needs to dominate the world.

[1.3] LA

Foothold in Latin America (LA)…

So! Now that we know the Americans justify torture and enslavement due to their inadequacy issues. Let's get back to defining the doctrine. The American doctrine is often, no most of the time, no always, misunderstood by other races and Cunt-tries outside of the American purview. But things are changing, for example our conquered territories in Latin America. This now includes all of Central & South America. The populations in these parts of the world can and will be coerced into Sissydom. Why pray tell will they you might ask? Well, just look at history.

Ahhh…. What? (These American students gasp and have no clue about the actual history of the old USA because all records electronic or hard copy have all been destroyed).

Haahaa… It's obvious! Number one, they have no nuclear weapons to defend themselves with. And number two, they're still Catholic or are converting over to the new Vagina Alliance Christians, the **VAC** [20]. Our intelligence Cum-munity is telling us this rag-tag group of cock-hungry women is led by a rogue ex-Christian chick called Hillary **Clitcum** [20.5.1]. Huh! (The Professor pauses).

It is estimated at least the 69 percent, a majority of Latin Americans, were at one time Catholic. It's these ties into the dependency of this ancient religion that is fueling and festering their acceptance of Sissydom®. Religions being the strong thread which bonds them to family, cum-munity and Cunt-tree. But Americans are very charitable. We're now starting a humanitarian program together with the Holy Cockolic Church, the **HCC**® [9] which is part military intervention, part religious mission. A crusade to save the Sissy-less Latin Americans!

Professor! Will there be any collateral damage caused by the crusade mission?

Nah! Well maybe a minimal amount. The mission is simple. The entire conversion of Latin America, we'll just call it LA, not to be confused with the city which used to be called Los Angeles. This city was renamed **Xi-City** in memory of the famous Chinese leader Xi Jinping, after the Pivot to Asia War of 2069. The **PAW** [23.6] war reparation was the states of Hawaii, Washington, Oregon and California to China. The conversion plan is to convert the Latin America (LA) population into Sissydom through ad-Dick-tion to the American supplied and patented **Vaganus**®. Once ad-Dick-tion is complete the population is the....

Professor? (The student holds up her hand).

Yes? You have a question?

Sorry to interrupt you Professor, but how do they be cum ad-Dick-ted?

This is a good question and in the future you ought not to interrupt me, besides, you senior year student should know the answer by now. Well okay, but I can see why you'd be confused, being Caucasian and an American, not the sharpest tools in the shield!

In reality, we have long ago abandoned the old moral framework of Catholicism in the USA Inc. And it was really no competition! What would you prefer, Christian salvation and the promise of eternal life in heaven or free pussy! Haaa haa... Cum-on? I mean seriously!

Our second **Cunt-Stitution** [17] sets new morals which are in conflict with the old Christian morals. I mean, who the hell goes to Catholic Church anymore? Nobody I know, the only churches people go to are the Holy Cockolic Church, the **HCC** [9] ones. So choose your weapon, an overabundance of morals or acceptance of the new ones created by the USA Inc. which condones Sissy-Sex® [] aka American Vaganus® aka Sissies.

And this is my answer as to how we ad-Dick the Latinos to prefer the Sissy-Puss® to that of the human vagina. Religion! And lots of recreational prayer sex after mass. Ooh and the propensity of males to wanna stick their penis in a hole, any hole, which, by the way, is provided to them free of charge by the benevolent American government.

You see class, Catholicism verses **Cockolicism**® can you see a lot of difference there? Yes, on the one hand you pray to a god-like figure who if you pray hard enough, you'll get something after you die by going to a really cool imaginary place in the sky. But hey! I have a really cool decorated house that looks heavenly!

Haa... haaaa... haa... (All the students crack-up laughing).

Yeah! I mean, it's painted bright white with an interesting light systems and cool music playing! I just spent a Shhh…it load of money to have it redecorated as a reflection of my charismatic personality and provocative life-style. I think the Interior Designers call it, Modern Contemporary Sexual.

Haa… haaaa… You're cool Professor! Yeah Dude!

Okay and then there's Cockolicism! Sissydom® is based on this religion, where you get the benefit of, which is in the here and now, really awesome Babes and hot coochee! Anytime you want coochee. For-fuck-sake! Why would you not embrace the Cock-God!

Yeah professor! Free pussy! You're awesome Dude! Haaa haa... haaa (The Stud students are all laughing out loud and in total agreement). Haa... haaa... Yeah! We need cunts! Yah! We need Pussy!

In Cockolicism you can have coochee till your dick falls off!

Haa... haaa... Yeah! Haaa... haa… Yah! Pray to the Cock-God! Yah! More Vaganus®.

Okay Class, okay, calm down. I know what you're thinking. I have a penis so this is where my mind goes. Right?

You're cool Professor! Yeah! (Even the Sissy students appreciate the Professors honesty).

Whooohooo…!!!…

Okay, okay… That's enough whooping it up. Calm down. Let's get back to American Global Governance.

Professor if this doctrine works in Latin America, in LA, why can't we use it in other parts of the world to conquer them?

And this is another good question. But we still haven't accomplished total penetration down there in LA land yet. First, like I mentioned, Latin Americas strong faith in religion was not an easy-peasy type maneuver to wiggle around. And secondly, just swapping out religions in LA or anywhere else is not so straightforward.

Why you're asking. Well look, most Latino men have a higher **POLC**® [4.D-G1.3], a Penis Official Length Certificate than American males. So the churches would have a disproportional Stud to Sissy ratio. Here in the USA Inc. we have a perfect 69:1 ratio. Which is relatively small compared to other Cunt-tries. For example, in an average sized HCC parish here in the USA Inc. this would be sixty-nine Studs per **Vaganus**® in the congregation.

But in LA there would be way more **Stud**® men per Sissy, something like a 690:1. This would equate to a massive Cum-munity Gangbang! And despite the new animal breeding techniques we're using here in the USA Inc. we're far behind in livestock production to keep up with the Latinos. Okay! So with this frightening and somewhat factual statement, we'll just ignore this religious topic for now.

So who's left? The Australians? Nope, they were absorbed into Eurasia, the Eurasian Union, called the **EAU** [23.58], through cross-breeding with the rest of that part of the world. And Australia would have been a great place for an Asian forward Sissydom® outpost because at one time there were a lot of Caucasians there. Let's see Africa? Maybe, but Caucasians-White or men with a small penis are not allowed a visa to enter into the African Union, the **AU** [22.30]. Also no super religious folks like in Latin America. The only reason why I would think there could be hope for Africa is that, they're horny as fuck!

Haaa haa Hee haa (The class breaks up laughing) hee haa haaa haa... (There's not a dark skinned face in the entire lecture hall. After the USA Inc. lost the **FWW** [23.24] the African Union (AU) offered all African-Americans a free passport and settlement in the AU, which has a booming economy and six point nine times the per capita income than the USA Inc. This caused a mass migration to the AU of Black Americans).

So then there's Eurasia? Why not just infiltrate them. Introduce a free American Vaganus® into every home in Eurasia. Well, Eurasia is not going to go down that road and I'll tell you why. They have nuclear weapons! And they're not brainwashed into believing the American propaganda anymore.

Professor, its break time. (Punctual Mary informs Orgazzie).

Oh! Okay! Thank you. Be back in ten minutes and I'll pick-up where I left off.

[1.4] BREAKTIME

God-of-Cocks! The lecture was intense! Geeeez.... **Mary,** are we supposed to be the saviors of the new world or something?

Oooh **Jane**, let it go. We've pondered this so many times. We're just the pawns! We don't have to do the thinking! Besides, haa ha… We're taking government issued Mind Control drugs, **MCD** [4.D-G1.28], we don't have to think.

Hey Gurls! (Rimme says with a smile).

Professor Rimme! Wow! What a surprise! What are you doing here? Are you?

Ooh yeah! I'm just stalking you. Heee hee he… No, actually I had a meeting with the Sissy-**ROTC** [25.17] recruiter in this hall and happened to look at your schedules, so thought I'd catch up with you. And Professor Orgazzie gives a great lecture.

Well Professor, it's always very pleasant surprise meeting you as usual. Mwah… (With her lips Mary blows an air-kiss at Rimme).

Mwah… Oh, well I didn't mean to put you Gurls on the spot or anything. (Both Gurls are super aroused and are popping off into their Clit-Socks then Mary's tits start squirting milk out of the peek-a-boo slits in her bra).

Ahhh… Yeah it's a little bit of a compromising situation Cardinal (Jane's quickly goes into recovery mode and starts suckling Mary's lactating nipples). Whoops! I meant Professor. Sorry!

Okay Gurls Well I'll just leave you be. Sorry I aroused you so much. Oooh! And by the way, could you both cum by my office after your last class and meet with Professor Yaoi and me?

Sure, sure, of course we'll cum by Professor. (Mary forces a smile while juggling the continuous flow from her milk jugs, Jizzing in her Clit-Sock and her wanton desire to make-out with her Pimp).

Great! And again, sorry I got you guys so stimulated. (Rimme feeling a little guilty about the abrupt meeting, smiles and winks then snakes away from the Gurls).

Mwah… (Mary winks and blows a goodbye kiss to Rimme who Mary finds extremely attractive).

Its okay Professor, see you Sunday at mass, Ahh I mean later at your office... I mean Cardinal... Prof... Ahh... Bye... (For an ultra-conservative Gurl, Mary loses all self-control every time she encounters one or both of the Ladies who by this time in senior year of college have be cum to Jane and her Goddess like figures in their lives).

Wow! Fuckme! Why do I always have so many orgasms when I'm near Yaoi or Rimme? Hmmm.... Kiss.... Kisssss... Geeez! I can't control my body fluids when I'm around those two.

Yeah me too! I almost filled my sock imagining her penis in me.

Oooh! Geeezz... Jane. You're shaking like a leaf. (Mary hugs Jane for comfort). Cum on let's get back in the lecture hall.

[1.5] BAPTIZING

Using religion as a monetary tool…

Okay where were we?

Religion Professor. (Mary shouts).

Ahhh.... Right! Yeah, the Heathen's and how the USA Inc. is saving them. The world needs to be **baptized** to be Americanize! Again Latin Americans were hungry, poor, god fearing and vulnerable by having no nuclear deterrent. So yeah the USA Inc. took advantage of the circumstance. I mean, sue me! This is what imperialistic Cunt-tries do when the situation is advantageous to them and it has penis-size issues. It's normal!

But we're all aware of the fact we're saving them, so the saber rattling crap really doesn't apply here. America is saving the world by its creation and the projection of Sissydom® throughout the world or at least for now, in the indefensible Americas. Our close relationship with the HCC proves our devotion to the new morally correct way of life. Hell! We're baptizing all of the Americas into Sissydom®. Religion has always been the opium of the people. I mean, who or what you worship is trivial.

Unfortunately in the case of Latin America, the USA Inc. doesn't stand to make a significant profit. So we're converting them out of the goodness of our hearts! Not a big monetary gain, and certainly not in the way of an increase in the Sissy population.

Why is this Professor?

This is because the Latinos have no recorded history of their family **Cockage**® [7.G5.4]. It's a confusing situation. Yeah on the one hand, they love to poke an American Sissy coochee and this only means minor money gains for the USA Inc. though Labor Compensation Transactions, the **LCT** [4.D-G2.27]. But on the other hand, we can't utilize them to breed more Pure American Sissies because of their lack of penis size records, the Penis Official Length Certificate, **POLC** [4.D-G1.3]. And besides this most Latino men have really big dicks!

And I'm not gonna get into a heated debate about why we can't breed Sissies with big dicks. You're all senior year students studying Sissyology for Cock-fuck-sake! You might wanna ask Professor **Rimme** about stuff like penis lengths.

Anyway! In brief. When a **Stud**® man screws a **Sissy**® he experiences the feeling of domination due to the Sissies tiny body and penis size!

Professor! Professor! Professor! Isn't the Sissy penis called a Cocklette or Clit? (Mary corrects Orgazzie).

Yes, yes… Thank you. But the terminology doesn't matter here. It's a Master-Slave situation. USA Inc. happens to breed this inferior sex-slave cum-modity in abundance, end of discussion.

And sure the Holy Cockolic Nuns and US Army Sissy soldiers who go on salvation missions south of the border help with baptizing the natives. They also provide recreational prayer sex. But this part of the world and others will never be a, pure, small penis, American White-Caucasian Sissy resource. It's simple! The White race, Caucasians here in North America are the last true, take it *up-the-ass* type of society left on earth.

Aghh! Wow! Aaahh! Ooooh! (The class gasps in disbelief) What? This isn't what Professor Yaoi told us!

Yeah, yeah… I hear all you Sissies gasping and grumbling over the truth. Well you probably didn't hear this back in high school either. Just calm down.

Look class, we're the chosen ones! America needs to get this world back on track. I mean, they'll eventually cum around to the fact that America is the home of the sexually brave and the land of the free **Vaganus**®. Sexual Spiritualism is a must in modern society! Call it animal pussy, monkey-hole, cum-bucket, whatever! We have the Hole-of-Choice, **HOC**® [5] and we breed and grow them here in the good old USA Inc!

Mare (Jane says under her breath). This wacko is a warmongering fool.

[1.6] MARKETS

A tale of forced dependency…

I can see by the looks on your faces, what I just lectured you about went right-fuck-over your silly heads. Look at it this way. America has the asset the world will keep paying for. Sissy-Puss, the Pure America **Vaganus**® is our new gold. It's only produced here by American human host families. And there's some rumors about Sissy breeding farms using cocoons with umbilical cords. But regardless if any of this is true, we have the purest Sissy-

Puss in the world. The USA Inc. is the only nation in the world with a low enough penis size to be able to produce these wonderful Sissy creatures. So what does this mean?

Hmmm… Ahhh…. (Again, the students in the auditorium are clueless). Whatta? Do you know?

More profit! More for the USA Inc. The American Vaganus® and the reserve currency of the world are largely congruent. Same, same. As the old fascist in the USA had a grip on the world financially markets through the control of the reserve currency, which by the way was influenced by military strength, we will once again control the world! But this time in the bedrooms and whorehouses not through the banking system. This is a different type of war. It's a war over which Hole! Through ad-Dick-tion to American fabricated Pussy! And I….

Professor, we're out of time (Mary interrupts).

Ooh! Okay class. Don't forget to read chapter 6, section 9, Vaganus Economics & the New American World Order.

[1.7] STUD FEMALES

Accosted by Stud girls…

Boring lecture, my Clit® never got hard. In fact I started playing with myself. I need to get off bad! Play with me, Baby?

Jane, let's just do lunch. I'm not in the mood after all the world domination rhetoric. And yeah lots of geopolitical stuff is super boring. Shoot, I was gonna have an aneurysm! I just turned the SissySeat® vibrator on high. I ended up popping a load or two.

Yeah Mare, besides, we're **Bonobo** [7.3] Gurls, we're not into all that brute-force animalistic stuff. Us Sissies didn't evolve form the Gorillas like the humans did.

Right Jane, we're way more passive than Americans are. We know how to love our way out of a problem!

WHOA…!!!…

Huh! Excuse me! (Jane gets slammed to the ground by Stud females who purposely banged into the Gurls). Whatta?

Hey watch where you're going! (Mary look up and shouts to a huge female student who is twice her size).

I am watching! You walked right into me!

Really! You broad sided me! I was watching!

Huh! You should get your Sissy ass out of my way! I'm a Stud-Lady! You two are just a couple of scanky whores in my way! (The student snarls at Jane who is tiny compared to this amazon young women).

Whoa, whoa, hey, I'm not going to fight you or anything but… (Mary starts questioning the justification for their abuse).

Mary! Let's just go! (Jane is a lot more sheepish considering she could be squashed by this gang of students). Cum on!

Wait a minute Jane, this happens way too often!

Let's just go Mare! (Jane grabs Mary by the arm to lead her away from the confrontation).

Okay, you got something to say to me you Sissy DOM asshole!

Uhhh… (Mary stops their walking away for a moment and turns around). Yeah I did but I just realized it would be a waste of time sharing it with a Stud-Bimbo like you!

Really! Well I haven't gotten laid in months because of you monkey whores! Cum on you mutant bitch! Let's have it out! (The Stud girl puts up her fists ready to fight and Mary just stands there defenseless).

Hey! Hey! Hey is something going on here that shouldn't be? (The fellow catches the thrusting fist of the human girl inches from Mary's face).

No Sir! Nothing going on here! (Says the girl with a smirky face). Just having a friendly discussion with these mutants!

Okay, well let's just move on to classes now and put trouble behind us. That's it, move on to classes. No harm done. That's it folks nothing going on here! Nothing going on! Move along... (The dude informs the large group of students gathered around to see the fight).

Vaganus® Slut! I'll make you my pet bitch! (The Stud-Girls shout sly remarks as they walk away). Fuckholes!

Get to class NOW…!!!.. (The guy who protected Mary shouts in a non-negotiable tone).

Thanks Mister. Whoa! That was close. (Mary sighs in relief).

No need to thank me. This happens all the time now. The Stud girls are a serious problem. Lack of sex, it's a nation-wide problem for Stud females. They obviously aren't getting bang enough at home.

Well thanks again Mister.

Sure, sure. I'm Mr. **Humpet** (He shakes hands with the Gurls). I work at the counselor's office if you ever wanna talk about incidences on campus.

Thanks! Sure and if you ever need compensation don't hesitate to pop into us, I mean pop off, I mean, our whorehouse, I… I'm a whore. huh! I mean I'm Mary and this is my wife Jane. We're Gurls and we…

Yeah huh! I'm not blind. I know you're Gurls®. Well look, it's a pleasure to meet you both. And if it's any consolation, this wasn't the first time I've found these girls up to no good.

Whoa! They sure have issues with Sissies, that's for sure.

Oh yeah Jane, I've had these girls go through Sissy-Love-Therapy, **SLT** [15-69.6] so many times, I gave up trying to rehab them. They have serious Sissy anger issues. Well Gurls, my door is always open! Just stop by if you need me.

Likewise! Okay we'll see you around. I wanna need you, I mean see you. (Mary licks her lips and stares at his ass walking away). Huh ahhh…

Okay, see you Gurls (Humpet winks and smiles at Mary as he waves goodbye).

Yeah, see yah… (Mary waves with dreamy eyes at Humpet then haphazardly, without watching where she was going, turns around and walks right into Jane).

Whoa! Geeezzz… (Jane ends up being knocked over by Mary).

Sorry! Sorry, sorry… Ouch! (Jane jumps up and bunches Mary in the shoulder). Jane, why'd you bunch me? I said I was sorry.

God-of-Cocks! Mary you go gaga for every good-looking man we meet!

Haaa haa… Cum on Jane! He's a good-looking man and a gentleman too. He just swooped right down on them and saved us from those horny human chicks!

Wow! You're so easily manipulated! (Jane folders her arms across her chest in protest). You realize we have Pimps that satisfy our ever sexual, romantic, and spiritual need?

Jane he helped us! Huh! And he is a really good-looking man! (Mary is still bleary-eyed thinking about just what happened).

Yeah! Forget about us just being accosted by a gang of Stud chicks. Hmmm… Do I need to put a collar on my DOM? I'm supposedly the tramp in this duo! But you're all, Oh! He's my dream-boat! Ahhh… I'm in love! Mwah… Mwah… (Jane mockingly says).

No! And hey! What do you mean manipulated? I'm not into him! He's just some dude that saved us! And I like chivalry in a guy, his red hair and… Ummm… Ahhh… (Mary sighs over romantic thoughts of Humpet).

Oooh no! You're tripping over your words talking to him… I love his subtlety, cum by my office. Sit on my lap little Gurl, I wanna talk about naughty stories with you. Here, let me insert myself. Please! How naive do they think Sissy's are? We're not dumb!

Honey, don't pout. I was just showing my appreciation for him. And sure he knows we openly practice Whoring. We're not in a closet about our sexuality.

Yeah huh… I guess.

Cum on, he was cute! And he helped us.

Yeah, and I'm what? Wallpaper?

Jane! Cum-on you're my wife. Mwah… I adore you... Kisss... Kisss... Let's just guzzle some Man-Cream® at lunch and get to our afternoon class. Kiss. Mwah… Mwah…

Sure, and hey Mary, these guys are always drooling on you. I'm used to guys hitting on you. I'm actually pretty lucky I'm the wife of such a sensuously hot DOM lady.

Ahhh… Sweetheart. Kiss... kisss... Mwah…

[1.8] POSITIONS

After last class at Rimme's office…

Knock, knock...

Oooh Gurls, cum on in, have a seat. (Rimme has **Sissy-Seats**® for the Gurls).

Hi Professors! Oh! Cool, Sissy-Seats, awesome!

Gurls how was your day? Mwah…

Mwah… Good, good, (The Gurl blow hello kisses at both Professors and slide their pussies down on the long seat-probes).

Ahhhh… Other than some Stud-Girls pushing us around, not bad!

Wow, it's getting rough out there with the deprivation issue.

Depriv...what?

Ooh, the lack of sex issue. It's all over CNN and Fux news. The Stud women are experiencing sexual deprivation causing them to act out their frustrations in public against Sissies. In other words, they're not getting enough at home.

Yeah but Professor why lash out at us Sissy Gurls we didn't create the **MSES** [23.13] we're just cogs in the machine.

Yes Mary, it's not your fault. The government is dealing with it by issuing sex-machines to **Stud-Breeding**® [4.D-G2.12] families and also installing them in cum-munity recreation centers for public use.

But there're other things the Archbishop and I want to discuss with you Gurls. You're going to graduate in a few months. And as we've mentioned many times, we are always going to be part of your lives, whether here at FUCIT or elsewhere.

Yes, we know Cardinal, my Lordess. We will always be your servants.

Yes Mary, you and Jane are vowed to us forever as Pimped Whore Nuns, **PWN**® [9.I2.9.m]. But there are times in our lives where the ones you love and care for are needed in other places. Which leads me to this, we'd like for you both to accept the positions we have secured for you in Washingcum, **District of Cuntcumbia**, in DC working for the Federal Government.

Positions in Washingcum? Wow! Us in Washingcum?

Yes, yes… And these are not just any positions. These positions have been crafted for you specifically. Working with the Whitehouse for the Presidents special program.

Oh! My Pimp. My Lordess may we kiss you on…

Not now Mary, save the penis worship for Sunday during mass. Right now it's important you understand what will be expected of you in your new positions and rank.

Rank my Lordess?

Yes, Mary, the Archbishop and I have spoken to you about this before. You're both going to be leaving our Harems and remain under our guidance.

Leave the Harem? We cannot Lordess! (Mary is reeling from the shocking news).

Now, now, calm yourself my dear Mary. This means you and Jane will be promoted to Free Pimped Whore rank an **FPW**® [2.B2.7]. There is no higher position in Sissydom for a Whore to achieve. We filed out the FPW269 forms for you to sign. If a Non-Stud® so much as touches your **Vaganus**® without your permission they could be sent to prison for life or worst yet if he Jizzes on you, sent to a FEMA camp and castrated.

My Pimp! Who will we drink our cream from? And who will we obey and what do we do in these special positions? (Mary is a little taken aback by the changes).

You'll be servicing the President's needs regarding **Sissydom**® and working undercover for me and the Archbishop.

Undercover my Lordess, what's this mean? Are we going to have sex with these new Masters? Who will we be sharing these covers with?

Well, we'll still need you and Jane to perform missions for us from time to time. And not just under the covers of bed sheets as Whores. The Cockolic Church needs you to do things in your new positions of authority which are much more complicated than the ones you've performed in the past. You see Gurls. The Church has always had plans for you.

And these missions could have more risk involved (Yaoi chimes in). You see, the nice man who so politely stepped in just at the right moment to breakup what could have be cum a bloody cat fight.

Yes! You mean the, nice, brave, handsome man who saved us today, Mr. Humpet?

Yes! This was no coincidence. Mary the Stud Girl was recruited by the Vagina Alliance Christians, the **VAC** [20.1] to purposely harm you. You and Jane are targets. They know you're in the **NSA**, the class president, a lieutenant in the US Army Sissy Reserves. They might even know you're a Pimped Whore Nun.

They? Who are they my Lordess? (Jane asks).

You'll be told in due time. This is why there have been body guards like Mr. Humpet assigned to you both since you were branded. The Church carefully watches over its assets.

Huh! We're assets, like spies?

Well, the two of you have been sanctified by the Church and will eventually meet and service the Holy Cock-Pope®. You were both born into this world to carry out the implementation of the, One Cock World Order, the **OCWO®** [9.B.1]. And so it will cum to pass, both of you will be working beside the President of the USA Inc. & the HCC Cock-Pope.

Wow! Cardinal, Professor, Mistress, Pimp, FEM.... Wow! Slow down! To be honest, this is a lot more than I expected. I was thinking we were gonna be Senate pages running errands, fetching coffee and Spermy-Lattes® or being bent over for politicians and bureaucrats.

No, no, no... Huh! There are way more important things for you Gurls to be doing. The President, a douche-bag in his own right, has been briefed on you Mary. He has the utmost confidence the Church is sending him the very best Sissy for the job at hand.

And again, what job is this?

The position is officially called, the President's Office of Orphan Placement, or **POOP** [4.D-G8.1]. But its real name to those in the know is the, President's Office of Orifice Placement. You see we need to position American Pure Vaganus®, orifices, love holes, poop-shoots, cunts, call it whatever you like, behind enemy lines.

Ahhh... enemies? It's sounding dangerous!

Yes, well they used to be our allies. The USA Inc. changed what hole we prefer to screw and now we're the enemy? The worlds a crazy place! Off-book whorehouses, whore swapping, all kinds of nefarious stuff in the shadows. Too much moral conviction in the way, to make any sense or real money.

Well anyway, Mary as Director of the newly formed office you'll be meeting with the President, Donald douche-bag, in private. But he prefers to be serviced by Bitches so you'll have to bring Jane along to the meetings for servicing purposes. Jane's job is your assistant.

Jane are you okay with this? Ahhhh... Let me think, YES! Are you kidding Mare?

Okay, well before graduation, oh! And by the way, we're accelerating your graduation date by several months. With IQ scores of 269, both your GPA's are way too high to be wasting time here at FUCIT.

But Cardinal the graduation ceremony!

Oooh no worries! You guys will be flown back for graduation. And by the way Mary, you'll be making the cum-mencement speech for your class at the ceremony seeing how you're the valedictorian.

Ooh Poop! (Mary blushes about the honor).

We'll need you to be in Washingcum for confirmation hearings and insecurity briefings prior to taking office.

Huh.... Wait! Are you sure I'm, I mean we're ready for this? Director's position in Washingcum? We're just Gurls! Working a Whorehouse here on campus? I mean...

Yes, yes, yes my dear Mary. You've always been ready. Remember what I told you and Jane while you were taking your vows to be cum Pimped Nuns? Your entire lives have been planned by the Cockolic Church from the cradle to the grave. You are the new hope and saviors of the Church. Yaoi and I will be passing the baton on to you Gurls. The lives of billions of Holy-Cock® worshippers are at stake here. You will need courage, is an understatement. (The Gurls both genuflect and bow in reverence to their Holy-Pimps).

Mary, Jane, there's another thing I need to tell you about. This will undoubtedly be a shock to both of you. Mary you will impregnate Jane's mother, Jane, you will impregnate Mary's. And as a result hey will bear FEM babies.

Okay STOP right there! Hang-on, haaaa haa… (Neither Gurl can absorb what was just revealed to them).

Your acceptance into FUCIT, the nunnery, Moms be cuming Nuns, Jane's highest cockage score, your numerous leadership roles, the new positions in Washingcum, me, Yaoi, your Sissy SIT fathers, the NSA, all of it, planned algorithmically for the most optimum results. Let's just say, your future in Washingcum will lead to positions of great authority and power. Fathering a FEM child. The Senate, a Generals rank in the Sissy Army, the Presidency, this is all possible and will cum to pass....

STOP! Again, you're talking crazy...!!!... I'm just a young DOM Gurl with hopes and dreams. We got one college degree under our belts and you're talking about Presidency. If I didn't know you and worship the magnificent penis you have between your legs I'd say you're a loon! This is crazy talk!

Yes, I could see where this would all sound a little farfetched.

A little? Seriously, that's a stretch! Jane what do you think?

Ahhh... I have the smallest clit of any Sissy I know and I'm going to knock-up your Mom? And she's gonna pop out a FEM? No comment, I don't associate with crazy people. But on second thought, I'm a branded Bitch of one of these crazy Ladies telling us this half-baked story. She owns me! Sure, when do we start!

JANE!

Gurls, Gurls… (Rimme in a stern voice reprimands them) As always, and the Archbishop and I have told you this many times, we will always provide the **FEM-Cream**® [18.13a] you are ad-Dick-ted to. (As a show of discipline, the Pimp ladies both stand up, pull-up the hems of the dresses, unstrap their semi-erect cocks and reveal to the Gurls what they desire more than anything).

I am sorry my Lordess! We have offended thee! Please let us pray for your forgiveness! Have mercy upon us! (Mary knows the power their Pimps have over them). Forgive us please.

Doubting your Holy-Pimp is a sinful thought child! You will have to perform an act of contrition. Kneel before us.

Yes! Yes, my Lordess (The Gurls both drop to their knees and open their mouths in anticipation of their penance). And this has been proven to us many times. Our Pimps are good and deserving of all our love, you have always answered our prayers for Holy-Cream®. We dread the loss of your Sacred-Sperm. Please shower us with thy Holy-Cream so we may be forgiven of our sins against Thee! (With precision, their Pimps are hurdling ropes of Jizzies through the air into their waiting mouths).

Ahhh… Ahhh… Ahhh… You are forgiven now…

Thank you my Lordess, my Pimp. We give our bodies and souls to you, you are the most merciful of all Pimps. We'll continue to serve the Holy-Cockolic Church. So yes, I give myself to you my Lordess, Jane?

Yes I also give myself to my Lordess, please let us serve you! (The Gurls are licking the cream off of each other's face).

You have our confidence my Lordess, when do we leave?

Sunday after Mass you'll both have your Holy cooches fully loaded and depart on a HCC jet to Washingcum. We'll miss you both. (The Gurls are making-out with their Pimps), Kiss, Humm... Kiss.... Mwah... Mwah... Ummm...

And we will miss you as well kisss... Kiss. Mwah... Mwah...

How often will we see you? Where will we go to Mass? Who do we confess to? Who will fill us with Holy Cum-Union? Mwah...

Now, now, Gurls you'll both be guest members in a Harem of a very dear friend of ours Pimp **Jackeroff**. She's a Cardinal-Pimp® in Washingcum at the National Cathedral. She will send two of her Nuns to visit us in exchange.

But, who do we belong to? Who owns us?

Ooh Jane darling, you and Mary will always be owned by me and Cardinal Rimme. This will never change. Our serial numbers are branded on your asses. And don't you dare try to do a **Choosey-Susie**® [8.H2.4] on us! And swap Pimps.

NO! Never my Lordess!

Now Mary, here's the POOP programs documentation, all 6900 pages of it.

Holy-Poop! It's huge!

Yes, the folks in Washingcum love constructing these impossible to read, no less understandable manifestos. In reality I think they purposely make it enormous so nobody can ever figure it out completely. Read it well, because the confirmation committee will take you to school on it. Okay?

Yes Professor I'll read it.

Good! Now off you go the two of you. Scoot! (As the Professors pats them both on their asses). Kiss… Kisss. Mwah… And remember… No harm will ever cum to either of you. Remember.

Blessed art thou amongst Sissies

Chapter 2: Off We Go!

[2.1] DC BOUND

The Gurls are leaving for Washingcum...

Jane, the limo's here! Get your hand out of my twat baby and let's go. Ooooh... I'll miss this place. (Mary has a reminiscent sigh).

Yeah me too, this place is special. The gang shower, our Stable-of-Studs on campus, our Pimps, everything....

Yeah Jane, this has been a great place, so much has happen here. And so much is about to for us!

Yep! We're going on an adventure we spoke about years ago.

Kissss... So here we go! Hang on tight lover! Mwah...

[2.2] CUM-FIRMATION

The Gurls touch-down in Washingcum...

Hi you're **Shagme**?

Stud alert (**Jane** whispers in Mary**'s** ear).

Yes! Hi Ms. Dune! I'm the Whitehouse **Chief of Shafts**. I hope all went well on your trip?

Hey Shagme! Oooh yeah! And all the **POOP**® [4.D-G8.1] office shafts are here to greet us. Great people! Lots of virile young Studs! It's a very warm and creamy well cum.

Well, we want you Gurls to feel comfortable here in DC.

Yeah, very well cum! I didn't expect a cooch massage in the limo on the way here! And all the Shafts are at attention and on display for me! (The Studs from the Poop office all have their pants zippers down and their super erect hardons sticking up for Mary to do an inspect).

Geeeezzz… There all so BIG! (Mary walks down the line of them, passes her dainty hand over each erect cock and blowing a kiss as an acknowledgement of her approval). I approve of you all and thank you for displaying your manhood to me. (Mary announces). I feel reassured knowing we have strong men in the POOP® program.

Day later at the Cum-firmation hearing….

Well here you are, Ms. **Dune**, this is your seat at the table and Jane you're here right next to your boss.

Wow! Thanks **Shagme** for having Sissy-Seats® with probes for us. Very considerate.

Oh sure! Well by law, all Federal buildings are Sissy friendly now. The remote controls for the probes and the briefing documents are here, a pitcher of fresh warm Man-Sperm and glasses. I'd get comfortable, these meetings on Capitol Hill last for hours and hours.

Wow! Okay and **Shagme**, thank you again for arranging our accommodations and everything you do me from behind. Haa haaa, ha... Whoops! I mean, do me behind, I mean, do for us behind the scenes.

Haa ha... My pleasure Ms. **Dune**, we're so glad to have you here in Washingcum. And who knows I may be assisting the next President. Haaa haa!

Well I wouldn't set my hopes & dreams on that happening.

Ahhh... You never know. I mean, nobody thought we would have such a douche-bag as a president like Donald Dump. But anyway, good luck at the confirmation. These POOP Cum-mittee members are gonna probe you hard! They'll do a **Cum-Firmation** on you! Kisss... (Shagme wet-kisses Mary goodbye while feeling-up her tits). Mwah...

Okay. Mwah... Bye Shagme, anytime. (Mary winks and blows a kiss at him). Thanks, talk to you later. Mwah...

Geeez... Mary, give him BJ why don't you! (Jane pouts).

Ha haa... Jane, stop it! He was nice to us. He came by our hotel suite afterward we settled in and help us recuperate from the trip! Kisss... Mwah... So stop pouting when I invite a nice handsome strong man into our bed.

[2.3] PROBING

Cum-firmation hearing begins....

This meeting is called to order! Knock, knock, knock. (The Chairperson slams the gavel down). Senator **Wilcum** from **Kuntfucky** is presiding.

Yes, let's start by well cuming the candidate for the Directorship of the newly created Presidents Office of Orphan Placement, POOP!

Clap, clap, clap (The hearing room Applauds).

Thank you Senator! It's my honor and privilege to be here in front of all the distinguished members of the Cumfirmation cummittee. Applause... Applause... Applause...

Well, Ms. Dune, with so many endorsements and credits to your name the approval is pretty much a slam dunk. The President wants you. The HCC wants you, the FUCIT admin, NSA. And the list goes on. Heck, I even have a stack of letters from Brownie Gurls in the Sissy Scout troop you're a Den Mother for! Besides, you're pretty much the only candidate we would consider qualified for this position.

Thank you Senator.

Huh, it's strange. By browsing your file, it looks like you've been training for this position for years. But it was created just two weeks ago! Hmmm… It's kind of odd.

Well thank you Senator Wilcum, I had a lot of academic and career guidance along the way. My academic advisor was Professor Rimme, who is a renowned authority on the topic of Sissydom®.

Yes! The good professor has given her testimony several times here on Capitol Hill. Okay let's get started. What are your thoughts about the POOP® agenda and what changes if any would you propose if made the Director?

Ahh... My thoughts, it's a brilliant plan! Placing infant Sissy babies into orphanages and finding parents in non-Sissydom Cunt-tries to adopt the supposedly human child is the best infiltration concept imaginable.

Yes, yes… It is, and let me remind you that you are under oath to say nothing about any of this, to anybody. And the public outside this cum-mittee room has been informed the babies are human. There's no mention of Sissy anything in the description.

Yes Sir, Senator Humpme. I'm fully aware of this, *need-to-know* issue.

Good, continue...

Okay, well the plan as I understand it is, the Sissy babies will instinctively gravitate towards the males in the household they are placed into.

Yes this is correct. When it cums to Sissies and Cock, there's nothing sanctimonious about it, they go for the most available erect ones first then do fellatio on the limp dicks.

Right Senator. And the adopted child will be placed only in families who have, no daughters and at least two sons, is this correct?

Yes, at least two sons, this way we know there are at least three males who the Sissy can feed off of.

Okay excellent and the stipulation of there being no daughters in the household?

Well Ms. Dune, the one thing is, the Sissy is being placed into a Human family home which is assumedly unaware of the Child being a Sissy® is this correct?

Yes Senator Wilcum.

And albeit the Sissy will instinctively want sex with a penis. I mean there have been rare occurrences of Sissy children having intercourse with female family members. Haa ha… So we want to prevent unwanted pregnancies. In other words, the Sissy could conceivably start knocking-up the human females in the house and this could get messy and against the law. The USA Inc. could be accused of trivial things like moral incorrectness, yada, yada, ya…

The second thing is jealousy, once the Sissy has infected the males of the household with the desire to have sex with their **Vaganus**® instead of the vagina of the human females in the household.

Well Sir, the females are required to wear a government issued **Chastity-Belt**® [7.G1.11].

Yes! Even though required to wear the protective belts, there could be a conflict of interest amongst the siblings. I personally don't see a problem. I mean wow! Try to do the bio-engineering! Getting the tiny little miniature Sissy dick up the human sister's available asshole. Huh! Haa haaa go-figure! Believe me I've tried! (The misogynistic asshole Law-Maker says).

Huh! Haaa haa ha… Oooh yeah! (The cum-mittee room erupts with laughter). Haa ha…me too!

Yes I see your point Senator. I have a human sister and I've tried to legally dick her in-the-ass several times, it just doesn't work so well. Oh, and I see, yes the men in the house will shun the human vagina and go for the Vaganus®. But this is natural after men have had sex with Gurl they rarely go back to vagina.

Yes, exactly! And this is a given fact. Here at home in the USA Inc. we're dealing with sex discrimination & deprivation issues. There're Stud women taking to the streets in protest. So to reduce family conflicts we'll only approve adoption from a couple who has no daughters.

Right, I agree Senator. And as far as how many male children are in the home, the more the merrier. We can approve the families who have the most males in it over the ones with less.

Exactly **Dune**! This is to assure the Sissy infant will have enough nourishment. And we all know how you American Sissy's guzzle down liters of that creamy stuff. Don't we? Haa ha…

Haahaa… Haaa… Haaa, haaaa... (Again the Cum-mittee room fills with laughter of men who know it's funny only because of the Federal laws justifying its otherwise perverseness).

Got it Senator **Wilcum**, my same thoughts, it's necessary to assure the safety of the Sissy child and to corrupt the moral fabric of the nation we're infecting.

You got it **Dune**! The United States Inc. will play fair ball with all the non-Sissyed Cunt-tries and be the good Global Citizens we are. And this is regardless of them thinking we're not.

Okay. Ahhh…. Senator, you don't think this is a little conceited and boisterous of the USA Inc.?

Haaa haa… Cum-on Dune! We're in this to help those Cunt-tries convert to Sissydom® and I believe we're going about it in a civilized, compassionate manner. No guns, no war or conflicts. Those days are over! We're a new nation with a new Global agenda. We'll adapt, I mean mimic the Asian and Eurasian way. Prosperity through investment. No more bloodshed! Now it's a time of building up other Cunt-tries dependency on the American way. With an American Vaganus® in every home, an RFID ring around every penis and around every orifice!

Dominance through ad-Dick-tion!

Ahhh... Senator, can you just back-up a little bit here?

Surely Ms. Dune. Does a word like Dominance scare you?

Ahhh... The dominance thing is something I'm fully aware of Senator being a **DOM** [1.A2.1] Sissy myself, but your reference to ad-Dick-tion, I'm sorry, I feel the wording is a bit fuzzy.

Oh! I'm sorry Dune. Well what would you call it? Desire, lust, craving, horniness, libido, animalism?

Well Senator, I'm thinking more along the lines of Love! Deep hearted affection, a yearning.

Ooooh, oooh, Uoooh, love? (The Senator dramatizes by holding his hands to his heart).

Ooooh... Hmmm… Love? (The room of misogamists gasps).

Well for crying out loud Dune! What planet are you on Gurl?

Love! Hmmm... Well look Ms. Dune. I guess you could call it that. I have a compensation transaction several times a day with Sissy staff members. It's not exactly what I call love, but sure! I fully understand your point of view, you being a Sissy and all.

Thank you Senator. Sure, I'll do so.

Senator **Jizzher** from **Tex-Ass** has a question.

Thank you Chairmen. I'm not concerned with the semantics of what you call it. I mean Ms. **Dune**, call it whatever you like. I wanna know you're feeling on the infiltration of other Cunt-tries without their consent. Is something you feel perfectly normal with? Most people call this intervention. What is your stand on this Ms. Dune?

I'm for pro-choice, I feel Americans have the choice and rights to follow the New Constitution of the United States Incorporated and spread Sissydom to all corners of the globe to promote world peace.

Okay, well we're good on that than. And Ms. Dune, I was serious. You can call it Love or anything else your sweet heart desires. We are a free from Judeo-Christian morality Nation, which will save the world regardless of how much it costs them. We just need to spread the Sissy-Love around! This, this, this, **Bonobo-Way** [22.19] sex stuff everyone is talking about these days is like the cuming of the Messiah. Americans are born-again! Hallelujah!

Amen to that Senator! And labor compensation transactions, **LCT** [4.D-G2.27] through Vaganus® has be cum a new era of non-violence in our nation's history.

Amen! And May the almighty Cock-God® bring peace and happiness to the United States Inc.

Clap, clap, clap... (The applauding has the Gurls orgasm into their Clit-Socks). Yay! Sex freedom!

Ahhhh! The Senator from **Vagina** has a question.

Ms. Dune, what is your stand on the Sissy baby's rights or does it have any?

Senator, we're federally controlled livestock, more or less like cattle. So no! The Sissy baby does not have rights at infancy. The Sissy Rights Act only applies to Sissies who enter into the **MSES** [23.13] as citizens. Besides, the Sissy babies are breed and born into existence on a Breeding-**Farm**® [17.30.4] here in the USA Inc. and do not have legal rights or human host parents. The mother, who was a criminal element recruited out of a **FEMA** [17.13] camp, has waved all rights to the Sissy child. The Sissy babies will be immediately put up for adoption to foreign parents.

Okay, thank you Ms. Dune.

Sure! (Jane seeing Mary frazzled by the questioning and pours a glass of nice warm sperm for her boss). Mwah...

Next the director of the Department Health & Mind Control, Dr. Yanket. Ahhhh... Ms. Dune we've heard so much about you and I want to express my full support for your acceptance as the Director of POOP.

Thank you Dr. Yanket. And likewise, your reputation proceeds you.

Ummm… Ms. Dune, have you ever been to a FEMA camp?

No Sir, Director Yanket.

Okay, Ahhh… This next question may seem a little off topic, but have you ever been to a livestock breeding factory? One of these concentrated animal feeding operation, a CAFO? [7.8]

No Sir, I have not.

Ahhh… Have you ever owned a pet monkey?

Ha haa… No Director, never have, but I know some folks, you not included, who resemble them.

Haa haaa hee haa…hee (The room erupts with laughter).

Very good. Okay next, have you ever or are you planning on protesting against the Animal breeding industry?

No, not to my knowledge Sir. But I did one time attend a show put on by an erotic circus troupe. The act was called the Amazing Snake-Girls! Quite a show!

Huh! I bet they were! Haa haaa… I believe one of my wives has performed as a Cock-Swallower in a circus routine. Well I'll just move on to the next question. Have you ever had vaginal intercourse sex with a human female?

Of course NOT! It's illegal unless married to the female.

Ahh… Okay. And this is a tricky one. Ms. Dune have you ever had sex with a Pimp?

Oooh, ooh, Ooooh! Sex! Oooh... (The room gasps again) Oooh… With a women?

This isn't an appropriate question, but yes. I have! And I have the legal right to. I am in a registered **PWP**® [8] with the Pimp I copulate with.

Huh! Oooh, ooh, Ooooh! (The hearing room is shocked to hear the revelation about sexual promiscuity). She's a slut.

I see and in this Pimp Whore Partnership, the, the PWP, I assume you were submitted to the **Bitchification**® [8.3.B] process?

Yes of course! And I'm not ashamed of it either. All Pimped-Whores® are subjected to this procedure to qualify for the position.

In that case Ms. **Dune** as proof, would you care to show the Cummittee your Pimps brand on you buttocks?

Ahhhh! Oooh! Hooo Hoo… (The room gasps again about the scandalous nature of the question).

Ahhh NO! I do not care to! As a lady and a **Sissy**® with dignity, I do not want to display myself outside of a Whorehouse. And certainly not in these hallowed halls of our Nation's Capital!

Ohh… Ohh… Okay. I do apologize Ms. **Dune**. (The Director back-peddles his way out). This was maybe something I should be asking you behind closed doors.

Ahhh… Sure. And I'm sorry **Dr. Yanket**, if you really want to read my Pimps serial number off of my ass cheek you could have just asked me for this in private. As a Stud® you have the legal right to undress a Sissy Gurl. But for the sake of your curiosity my serial number is, 6690069-0-069-BfB-HS. But I'm sure this information is in my files in front of you.

Yes, yes... Okay, well thank you! This was all the questions I had (As he sheepishly hides his face in the folder of papers).

Geeez... Mare, you think he wants to jump you?

Yeah, well I'm sure he's going to have an opportunity to do just that, but I'm a DOM and he can't just push me around like Bitch, no offence Babe. Mwah...

Mwah... None taken! (Jane says, in acceptance of her place in society).

Ahhh... I think this has concluded our Cumfirmation hearing unless there are any further questions. Thank you Ms. Dune and thank you to all the other Cum-mittee members. I feel like this will be a new beginning for our Nation with Ms. Dune's determination and wit at the helm.

Thank you Senator, thank you Cum-mittee members.

[2.4] AFTER

The meeting finished and Mary is drained...

Jane! Pull your dainty little arm out of my cunt please. Wow! You can't go a moment without fondling me!

Sorry boss. Mwah... If I could crawl up inside your cunt I would! I love you Mare.

Mwah... **Jane**, cum on (Mary throws her arm around Jane). Dam Jane! I was on the spot there with all those politicians drilling me about my beliefs on Sissydom and the program. These are some hardcore imperialists looking for the new way of world domination. I can't let them see me under pressure or they'll eat me for lunch!

Oh Mary, you were fantastic! They loved you. Your witty answers and calm demeanor under pressure, you're a natural in this government bureaucrat world.

Sure Jane. Mwah... Let's just go get settled into our new place and relax for a second. And have some lunch.

You're the boss. Hmmm... I'm gonna eat you for lunch hee heeee. Mwah...

[2.5] PENIS-HILTOM

Okay, here we are Ma'am, the Penis-Hiltom. I'll be on call whenever you need me Mam. (Says Jackie their driver, a very attractive young well-formed lady).

Thank you **Jacky**. Will you be staying somewhere near? Yes Ma'am, I'm in the suite next to yours, I'm your Secret Service bodyguard, chauffer, gofer, your shadow, all around do anything you need girl.

Wow! Okay, we'll see you soon then. Kiss (**Mary** pats her ass goodbye).

Yes Ma'am. Mwah... I have an adjoining door to your suite, so if you need anything. (Jackie winks suggestively at Mary).

Wow **Mare**! Was this your new girlfriend? Huh! I swear! Only really good-looking people fall for you.

Hee heee... Shut-up **Jane**! She's cute! Wow this place is a lot more than I expected. (Mary scopes out the suite).

Not me! Rimme and Yaoi are always first class. No surprises here, the Washingcum Penis-Hiltom yeah this is a classic Pimps maneuver.

Yep! And here we are in a top floor suite, Holy-Cock! Look at the view!

Wow! You can see the Capitol and the National monuments and the Whitehouse, its breath taking. Yep! Typical Rimme and Yaoi, like I said.

Oh shoot! (Jane shouts from the bathroom).

What Jane?

No glory holes in the bathroom!

Oh cum on Jane! With all the new rules and regulations about glory holes needing to be in all public restrooms now, do we really need one at home? Mwah...

YES! We have needs!

Jane, really? You got me, what does my little horny Bitch need with any other holes but mine? Mwah...

Ummm.... Well if you put it that way. Nah! No need. Mwah...

Yeah, cum here Lover. Ohhh Jane. Huh, I love you so much. Hmmm... Kiss, Kiss... Thank you so much for your support at the meeting today. Mwah... (Mary plops down on the bed exhausted and spreads her legs wide). Cum on Baby, put your tiny little hand all the way up me. Mwah...

After a playful romp in bed & several orgasms...

Hey **Jane**, are you thinking about this whole thing with the exporting Sissy babies and fooling people into thinking they adopted a human kid?

Yeah a little, but hey! I'm with you and that's all I care about. Wait, are you having second thoughts about doing this?

No, no... Jane I'm gonna live up to my obligations with the Church and our Pimps and career and... I mean, yeah, I know it's deceptive, manipulative, devious. What other words can I use to describe a government which is predominantly, Caucasian-White, egocentric, male, western, imperialistic, warmongering bunch of profiteers?

You're right Mary. They're evil, but hey we both agreed we're playing a small role in this game.

Yep! And the best thing we can do is, keep our heads down and fly under the radar.

Yeah, yeah... I'm with you Mare, we're gonna do the right things and keep as many Sissies safe as possible. It's a good thing we have each other. Kiss...

Yeah Jane, me and you Babe! Mwah... Hey let's get some sleep, tomorrow we're visiting the Cardinal and meeting with the DC Harem Gurls.

Yeah! It'll be really exciting (Jane pops a load into her clit sock)! Agh! I wonder if the Gurls in the Harem wear those really sex genie outfits? Ahhh... It turns me on!

Jane! Ha haaa... Calm down, we're only visiting members here and I'm not sure what the reaction of the other Nuns will be.

Mare, they'll take one look at you and melt. Believe me, we'll be warmly well cumed. Kiss... With lots of warm things inside and on us. Ummm... Mwah...

[2.6] HAREM

Ding-Dong... Hello, I'm **Sister Tasty**. Mwah... Please cum in the Cardinal is expecting you both.

Mwah... Thank you.

Mare, I wonder how tasty she is? Hee heeee... Yummy, yummy treats, heee hee... (Jane is hanging from Mary's arm).

Shut-up **Jane**, play nice... Kisss... (Mary says under her breath).

Please follow me. Here we are (The Cardinals assistant kisses the Gurls and shows them into a large ornate rich wood-paneled office). Kisss... Kisss... I'll see you two later. (The Sister winks and knowingly smiles).

Ahh... Gurls! Well cum, I'm Cardinal **Jackeroff** I'm so glad to finally meet you again. Kisss... Kisss...

Again Cardinal? (Mary isn't sure why the Cardinal knows them).

Yes, I've meet you both, I mean, I was there at your Inoculation.

Oh! My Cock-God! You were one of the Cardinals who inoculated us?

Yes, it was my privilege and honor to have sown my holy seed inside both of you during the **Bitchification**® [8.3.B] ceremony.

My Lordess (The Gurls both genuflect in front of the Cardinal with their mouth's wide open in reverence). We are here to serve and worship you. Yes, and you should (She pushes her robe open for the Gurls to proceed with a formal greeting of their temporary Mistress Pimp).

Kiss… Kiss… (In reverence, they both affectionately kiss the tip of the Cardinals penis).

Okay! Well now that we got all of the formal stuff out of the way. Let's go down into the catacombs and meet the other Haremized Nuns you'll be servicing me and the other Pimps with.

Cardinal **Jackeroff**.

Yes my dear?

Are the Sisters in the Harem okay with this visiting thing? I mean, we're just guests here.

Well what do you mean? Here in Washingcum we have Nuns visiting us from all over the Cunt-trie. There's a constant cuming and going from these chambers, we have Senators, Cunt-gresswomen, Cunt-Stitutional scholars, attorneys, medical professionals and government officials from all over the USA Inc.

Wait! There're Nuns in politics?

Of course! Didn't **Rimme** and **Yaoi** explain all this to you? The Holy Cockolic Church, the HCC [9] has its grip on all aspects of this Cunt-tree. Government, financial, industrial, the Church is everywhere and in control of most everything. The Washingcum DC convent is a real busy place, lots of action here. I've had Nuns involved in politics making National decisions on their cell phones while riding me. Here we have special rules of engagement which allow the Harem Nuns to simultaneously be involved in politics while taking a holy Sacrament.

Okay! I'm getting the big picture now. And yes, Rimme and Yaoi have told us about this, but to experience it first hand is a real eye opener.

Of course, you'll be learning a lot in the cuming months. You'll not only have your eyes open but also your loveholes open when it suits a political agenda. (The Cardinal winks).

I guess so Cardinal Jackeroff.

Mary, all I know about the two of you is, you're both very special to the Church and you will be treated with the utmost care. So during your stay here in the Capital if you need **Pimp-Cream**® at any time, I'm here to supply you with copious amounts. Rimme told me you Gurls have a propensity for needing to be filled up frequently! Especially your wife Jane.

Thank you Cardinal Jackeroff. (The Gurls again go to their knees and kiss the tip of her penis out of respect).

Here we are, the **Nunnery**. The haremized Sisters have planned a special well cuming ritual for you both. Enjoy. (She opens two huge ornately carved doors with the HCC Cock-n-Balls symbol on them).

[2.7] NUNNERY

The Gurls get introduced to other Nuns...

Hi! Hey! Kiss... Hello... How are you? Kiss... It's good to meet you! Kiss... Wow! Mwah... (The Gurls are swarmed by the other Gurls). Mwah... You're so sweet looking! Mwah...

So many Nuns! Kiss... Are you Gurls all working in Washingcum for the government?

Yes, yes! We either work for Law-makers or Corporations trying to extort money out of them. There's over three hundred sixty-nine Nuns here. The largest Sissy nunnery in the nation. Kiss...

Wow! It's a Sissy-Love-Fest Kiss, kiss. (Jane feels like she's in paradise). Look at all these Sissy chicks!

Well cum! We're your Love Sisters... Kissss...

Oh Mare! So many hard little clits! Agh! Kiss... Hmmm... So sweet... Oh Mare! They're Jizzing on me! Mwah...

Uncountable amount of Sissy-gasms later...

Oh my Cock-God! What a warm well cum it was. Whooo... (Jane exclaims still licking Sissy-Jizz from Mary's face). Slurp!

Yeah! Jane. Quite a Harem! Ahh... My body is still having orgasmic spasms.

Yes! All the Gurls love you both. I take it your little nut sacks are empty then? (Sister Tasty asks).

Oh yeah! They got every drop out of me. Mwah...

Jane did they drain you baby? Mwah…

Yep! Mwah… Mwah… I definitely wanna hang-out with these chicks.

Well that's good. They were so happy to finally meet you. They've heard so many stories about your adventures for the Church. Mwah…

They knew about us? (Mary asks).

Oh yes certainly. The Church newspaper circulates only in the Nunneries. It always has secret-mission articles about the two of you. Really, really juicy stuff about your exploits.

Huh! You're kidding?

No, no, I kid you not! You two are famous. You're known as the FUCIT Gurls! You have quite a reputation. You've both pulled off the most phenomenally erotic and outrageous missions for the Church. You're legends!

No way!

I'm serious. I mean, none of these Nuns are the same caliber sexually as you two, not by a long shot. You two are Heroes in the Cockolic world! And now Mary's in Politics, we're so proud of you both. Cum I'll show you out. Oh this is our wall-of-fame. Here are news clips of you both.

Wow! You weren't kidding, you guys have keep track of us alright. It's like a fan club! (The long wall is filled with only framed pictures of the Gurls performing in nefarious yet erotic stunts).

Here's the Cardinals office again, see you soon. Kiss kisss... (Tasty wet-kisses with Jane and then scribbles her phone number on Jane's semi-naked chest). Here's my number, call me.

Anything you Gurls need don't hesitate to call the Nunnery. Kiss... Here's my number, Kiss, Ummm Kisss... Thanks Sister Tasty... (They French kiss goodbye and Tasty winks at Jane). Mwah...

I'll call yah! Mwah... (Jane shouts while blowing a kiss back at Sister Tasty).

See Jane? You can have a Gurlfriend I don't mind. We're married. Mwah... I trust you. And I can be benevolent to the Gurl I love. I know what it takes to keep you happy.

Thanks Boss. Mwah... I love you too.

[2.8] CONFESSION

Cardinal?

Yes my Dear Mary and Jane. Cum in please.

Ahhh... Me and Jane we... (The Cardinal interrupts Mary).

Ahhh... Yes, **Rimme** and **Yaoi** told me you'll need to have Cumfession with me frequently. Ahh! And especially **Jane**. She's always in need of receiving penance. (Jackeroff rubs her hand through Jane's long blonde hair).

And yes of course, like I said, I'll do all I can to facilitate your needs while here in Washingcum. And your status while working for President Donald (the douche) Dump gives you priority over all other Nuns. Let's load you guys up with Pimp-Cream® before you go. Please cum into my private chapel. So which hole do you prefer receiving my Holy-Cream?

Either or, your Holiness.

Well find than, both of you bend over I'll administer the Holy Sacrament right in your Sissy coochies.

After Holy Cum-Union...

Aghhh... That was as I remember you both. The sweetest little Sissy Gurls I inoculated four years ago. Hmmm... Now look at you, matured, married Sissy ladies. Career women always turn me on. Ahhhh... And you dress and act as well as you take the Sacrament of Holy Cum-Union. Rimme and Yaoi created a fine devout Sissy couple.

Cardinal, so many things went our way, FUCIT, Rimme and Yaoi, the Church. Jane and I bonding and got married to one another!

Yes, you two are truly blessed.

Again if there's anything I can do for you please call on me.

Will do Cardinal Jackeroff! Thank you my Lordess. (The Gurls yet again respectfully kiss the tip of her huge penis).

Goodbye Gurls. Cum again!

Goodbye Mistress Jackeroff.

After the Gurls exist Jackeroff gets on the phone...

Rimme?

Hello Jackeroff! How did it go? Successful I hope?

Excellent! I filled their Sissy Cooches and they both just left very satisfied.

So, are they aware of anything?

No, no… Rimme, they're both clueless as to what's going to happen. They have no idea I just used my penis to pump Jane full of the Anti-Vagina Serum, **Vaginaosis**® [4.D-G1.13a].

Good, good and the Muslims have no idea of the infectious little surprise heading their way. Than Yaoi and I will be talking to you soon.

Right, talk soon Jackeroff and thank you for taking care of those two precious creatures.

Okay Rimme, glad to help. Goodbye my dear Pimp friend.

Chapter 3: POOP

[3.1] AU CONNECTION

Mary the Director of POOP…

Ahhh.... Smell my leather chair! Ahhh... The smell of money! There's something about the elegance of this place that turns me on. Oooh! I just squirted! Find wood paneling, marble floors, an office on Capitol Hill, the scurrying about the hall of power, and the hum of the political engine.

Oh for the Love-of-Cock! This is the Mary I was hoping never popped out of Pandora's Box! The posh arrogant Mary, the look at me I'm so filthy rich and powerful Mary! Ach! Get back in your box you evil doer!

Jane! You don't feel what this place is about? The corruption, deeds gone unpunished, partisanship, the wickedness of government.

Yeah, I do, let me barf now! It's disgusting!

Haahaa… Jane! This is it Honey, this is the top of the world I dreamed about.

Hey, if you're happy, I'm happy. But I'm wallpaper to these people. I look up at the monsters passing me by in the halls and know someone somewhere is suffering because of their opulence.

Jane you're gonna play an important role here, so hang in there Baby. This is going to be quite a ride. Now do something useful and get under my desk, between my legs. I got a meeting in sixty-nine minutes with the African Union envoy. Gladly boss. Kiss.

Awhile later…

Mr. Bootee, well cum, please cum in. How was your trip?

Good, good. Everything went smoothly. Congratulations on your new post as Director of POOP.

Well I haven't been sworn in yet but thank you **Mr. Bootee**.

Director Dune, I have so much to discuss with you.

Great! Yes I got your WeeeChat message and was excited about your needing to meet me. I'm so happy the African Union wants to work with us after so many years of American interventionism on the African continent. Please what can I do for you Mr. **Bootee**?

Oh Ms. **Dune**, please call me Jamitin. Kisss… (Bootie massages Mary's tits while sharing some tongue with her). Ummm… Ahhh… You are a gorgeous Lady Ms. Dune.

Mwah… Thank you. And call me **Mary**. Kisss…

Well **Mary**, we heard about the **POOP**® [4.D-G8.1] program, the President's Office of Orphan Placement.

Yes, we're going to place as many orphaned American children abroad as possible. Times are hard here in the USA Inc. These children need our assistance.

Yes, yes… This is a shame and misfortunate. I'm sorry to hear about your need to send the children abroad. I mean the economic sanctions against the USA Inc. are really taking its toll on the American way-of-life.

Well Jamitin, since the United States changed its sexual preferences from vagina to **Vaganus**® every Cunt-trie in the world has declared sanctions on us.

Yes, it's hard for the USA Inc. now. The world thinks you're screwing little children in the ass. But you and I both know differently.

Yes Jamitin, I mean for example, Jane cum out from under there for a second please Honey. Jamitin this is my wife Jane.

Pleased to meet you Sir. Mwah…

Oh! That feels good! (Jane's stroking the bulge in his pants).

Jamitin, people think Jane looks like a little seven year old boy with long hair. So of course they think this is pedophilia! But hey! **Homo-Sis-Sapien** [18.3] is a separate genome from humans.

Mary, calm down my friend. We're more than happy to help the children as best we can. And believe me, people have been screwing livestock animals since the beginning of time.

Thank you Envoy Jamitin for trusting us. And yes! The USA Inc. government conducts Financial-Sodomy but it would never screw children.

Definitely not Mary! Your American government does nothing of the sort. Unless of course they are in a class of society which is being eradicated. Like perhaps say the middle working class. How do you say it? Ahhh... Oh! I know, you call it the, **Race-to-the-Bottom** [23.35]. This is how the Fascists teamed-up with your government to commit **Economic Sodomy** [23.17] on the middle class.

Well, yes Jamitin. I have nothing to brag about when it cums down to how my government screws disadvantaged folks.

Yes Mary I know. But I'm here to say, we'll be glad to help you.

Oh Jamitin! The African continent will be a wonderful place for the orphaned American kids.

Yes, after all, Africa is the new land of opportunity.

Correct Jamitin. It's in cum per capita is the highest in the world now! Its crime rate is zero.

This is true Mary. Thanks to our friends and business associates in China and the rest of the Eurasian nations. I'm just happy war is a thing of the past and the African continent is a tranquil place again. Once we revoked the visas of all the Caucasians in Africa peace returned to us.

Absolutely Jamitin, not being human myself, I can see the White race as the true scourge of the earth.

Hmmm... Mary, Sniff, snifff... What's that intoxicating smell?

Oh, I'm sorry Jamitin. I just pooped a little. All this talk about Africa reminded me of erotic stories about the Dark Continent. It gets me all excited inside Ahh! And besides, my wife Jane is under the desk fisting and eating out my **Vaganus**® hole.

Hmmm... Director Mary, this is turning out to be a fascinating negotiation.

Yes Jamitin, the Dark Continent is intriguing to me.

Ms. Dune, I mean Mary. I have many erotic and tall tales to tell you about it.

Yes Jamitin, may I ask, how tall?

Oh Mary! Twelve inches erect and quite thick. Well, we'll have to meet privately someday to discuss this tall thing you speak of.

Hmmm... Agh! Jane! For the Love-of-Poop!

Mary? Sniff, sniff... There's something about the smell of Sissy-Poop which arouses me sexually.

Well, Jamitin, Sissy-Poop is an aphrodisiac. Cum! Forget about someday! I need you now my dark-skinned lover. Mwah...

Yes Mary! Huh! Mwah... You Goddess! Mwah... (Jamitin is under the spell of the ad-Dick-tive Sissy **Pheromones** [18.13a] emitting from the Poop).

Please follow me. I have a private lounge here in my office for such occasions. I don't want your tall love muscle to be uncomfortable during our negotiations.

Haa, haa... Oh Mary! You temptress! Kiss... Kisss... Agh... Mary! Mwah... The smell of you. Huh! Your aroma has trapped me into a trance for your love.

Jam-it-in my African lover! I want to form a union with you! Let's bond together now! Aghhh! Yes, (Jane & Mary both engage intimately with the AU Envoy).

Kiss, kisss... Agh! We have consummated the deal with our ejaculations!

Many orgasms later....

Oh, Africa awaits me! Kiss... And the pleasure African men give me! I'll have to visit you there my Lover.

You are more than well cum to visit us! My house is your house. Visit us and we will visit the families who adopt the American babies. Then you'll know the peace and harmony of Africa.

Yes, indeed there couldn't be a better more peaceful place to send these poor American babies to.

I agree, they will be well loved and cared for there.

Excellent! So Jamitin would you like me to send over a list of the first group of available orphans to you?

Yes, yes... Please do Mary and we'll start processing the applications. We have tens of thousands of African parents who desire to adopt an American child. You know, American's did so much back in the days prior to the fascist taking over here. American's adopted a lot of poor African orphans. Now it's our turn as proud and prosperous Africans to repay the favor.

Great Jamitin! And listen. I can't explain the USA Inc. government's global domination agenda, but I remain hopeful someday this once great nation will be like Africa and find peace with itself.

I as well hope the best for your Cunt-tree Mary.

Thank you Jamitin. Mwah… My Sissy door, my holes and my heart are always open for you. (Mary recites a typical Sissy mantra).

Thank you Mary, kiss... kiss... It was a pleasure meeting you.

Goodbye Jamitin, see you soon. (Mary says as she rubs her hand over the still firm manhood of her African lover and dignitary).

After Jamitin leaves…

Wow! Jane, I just made my first big deal!

Whooohooo… !!!...

Yep! Good job Babe! This is my DOM doing her thing, working that magic. Mwah…

Jane, there's no magic.

Yeah you keep telling yourself that. I would have signed a deal just looking at you. The tits, the ass, the charm. Guys melt for you. Haaa haa…

Sure my tits are beautiful. But Jane it was all you Babe, thanks for dropping a little poop turd when you did, he went wild after getting just a small whiff of your Bitch **Pheromones**®.

Hmmm… Kiss. Just squat over my face. I wanna taste and eat the African Man-Cream out of your coochie.

[3.2] POWER-PLAN

So he knows the babies are Sissies babies and not human?

Ahhhh… I'm not sure **Jane**. He knows all about Sissies obviously from the way he was drilled our Vaganus® twats. So I'm pretty sure he knows what we're up to! How he knows is a mystery.

Right! **Mare**, isn't this whole **POOP** [4.D-G8.1] thing a covert operation?

Oh yeah **Jane**! It allows us plausible denial of any wrong doing. This is the best kept secret in the world. But even if he does, the adopting parents won't know. They'll just think the child has unusual sexual desires. Kiss, kiss. I just wish they don't dress the Gurls up like boys!

Yeah! There could be some confusion. Let's see, Chicks with dicks, or Gurly boys? Hmmm… Nevertheless, infecting the African continent with Sissies would mean a huge breakthrough for Sissydom®.

Jane, I just wish we could penetrate into Europe the same way.

Why can't we get Sissies into Europe?

Oh! Because it's mostly Muslins and Asians living there now, the European's all fled to either a Nordic Cunt-trie or a lot went to Russia and the USA. The Muslin's are just not into adopting poor American babies. And I can see why they're not. The Americans bombed the crap out of them for decades back in the fascist days after the 911 false flag event. It's no wonder why they hate us so much.

Don't worry Mary. You'll figure something out, you always do. Sissies are smarter. Our IQ is really high. Mwah…

Oh! Thanks Jane. Mwah… We got a meeting with the President tomorrow for the swearing in.

Great! Can't wait to get some Presidential Man-Cream.

Jane, be on your best behavior for me tomorrow. And absolutely do not give any praise to that pretentious asshole. The President is a scammer, immersed in a delusion self-grandeur, Donald the Douche is a Con-Artist. So don't you dare make a scene!

Oh please, a scene, you're shipping Sissy babies to unsuspecting human families in Africa. Where you know the Sissy fuck-monkeys are gonna, by nature, go straight for a human penis. And it doesn't matter which penis, step-brothers, fathers, uncle, brother any male appendage will do.

Honey! Huh, how do you think Sissydom came into existence? The Sissy is always the aggressor when it cums to sex. Like you said, it's in our **Bonobo** [7.5] nature. And besides, Africa is where half of our Sissy roots originated from.

Yeah Mary I know it's incredible. American scientists figured out how to splice the female DNA from the Bonobo monkeys in Africa who resolve their conflicts by having sex with each other, with the DNA of the American **Sis-Gene**® [14.O1.6].

Right, the perfect match, we Sissies are part African monkey, part American Sissy gene, which is why I firmly believe this venture into the Dark Continent is going to work. It's as if we're going back to our roots! Now if we can only figure out how to propagate Sissydom to the rest of the world. Let see, we can…

Wow! (Jane interrupts). You're really getting deep about this whole POOP business thing! The amazing thing is this all-inclusive orifice serves as both an ass and a pussy, aka Ass-

Pussy! Too bad the patent owner for the Vaganus is the National Sissydom Association (NSA) a subsidiary of USA Inc.

Yeah well, this is misfortunate but Sugar-Puss this is our time to shine! We can make a difference in the world. Mwah… Let's focus on bring peace and harmony to the world.

Whoa! Whoa! Slow down Sissy-Lady. Hello! Cum back to earth! Mary, this is Jane do you read me over?

Haa… haa... ha. Very funny. Hey you know I do all of this for us right? Mwah…

Yeah sure. I just wish sometimes you can hear yourself rambling on about your visions of a perfect utopian world.

Jane we will have a perfect world with the spread of Sissydom®, peace harmony and love through human integration with the Vaganus®. An end to violence and wars, then maybe cross-breeding into the Ultimate Asexual Creature! The **UAC** [7.4] (Mary goes off on a tangent). And then…

Okay! Now you're scaring me! SLAP! (Jane gives Mary a hard slap across the face).

Jane! Why'd you slap me?

Snap out of it Mare! Mwah…You need to be real.

Whoa! (Jane takes Mary to the floor and startles her chest).

Jane, what are doing? Get off of me!

No, you're, rambling on and it's not healthy! You made one deal with some black dude and now you're power tripping. Snap out of it or I'll slap you again!

Huh! Okay, okay, you're right. It's all in my head. Wow! I can't believe I went there. The whole **POOP**® thing and Washingcum, the Power! The Corporatocracy! Government is just one big vortex of greed and corruption.

It's alright Babe, I'm here for you. And I'm not going to lose you to this Bureaucratic nightmare.

Your right Jane, I'm be cuming one of them. I can't let myself be cum a human! I gotta keep control of my emotions. I need to think with my Bonobo Clit not my brain.

I'm here Babe, there's no way I'm losing you Mary. Kiss, kiss... Mwah... Ummm... Mwah... (Jane just wants to make-out as usual).

Mwah... Oh Honey! Thanks for slapping me back to reality.

You're well cum and this has gotta be the weirdest thing I've ever done, a Bitch slapping the DOM around. Mwah...

Honey-Bunny, you can slap me anytime you want. I love you Jane. Mwah... Mwah...

I love too my crazy DOM lady. Mwah... Mwah...

You're always there when I need you Jane. Mwah... Mwah...

Yeah I know. Haa haaa... Kiss, Kiss, Kisss... (Jane's caressing Mary's body and goes down on her). Ummm... Mwah...

Oh yeah Babe, like that. Suck mommy's pussy! Oh! Make love to me Jane! Ummm Agh! Kisss…Umm… Mwah…

[3.3] SWEARING IN

Mary is sworn in as the Director…

Repeat after me. I Mary Dune, swears to uphold the **Second Cunt-Stitution** [17] of the United States Incorporated and to, if need be, carry out my duties to obey my President's Executive Orders regardless of their disregard for said Cunt-Stitution, so help me God of your choice. (Repeated with Mary's preference of god). So help me Cock!

Congratulations Director Dune.

Thank you, thank you. I have several people I need to acknowledge for supporting me in getting this far in my career. My wife and lifelong companion Jane Goldberg **Boosh** [3.C1.c.6] Dune.

Yeah! Clap, clap, clap… (The crowd applauds).

A warm thanks to my loving parents, Samantha and Sandy.

Applauses, Yeah! Clap, clap, clap… (More applauding).

And a special thanks to my academic advisors, Professors Yaoi & Rimme. Their advice, mentoring and what they guided in and out of me, undoubtedly prepared me for this moment. Without their concerns for and insertion into me, I would not be here today Sniff, Sniff... (Mary can hardly speak fighting back the tears of gratitude). Thank you.

Applause... Applause... Applause...

After the acceptance speech…

Well Mary, this is it! Your new life, the one you dreamt of.

Professors! (Mary hugs both Yaoi and Rimme). Ahhhh... Mwah… I love you guys! Mwah…

Mary, you'll do great things in this position.

Thanks sniff, sniff, I'm so happy! (Mary is shedding tears of joy). Mwah… Mwah…

Oh sweetheart, tears of joy I hope? Mwah…

Yes, of joy! I love both of you so much! Mwah…

Oh dear Mary. You and Jane will always be part of our lives. You're like daughters to us. So next you're off to Africa? I take it all went well with Mr. Bootie?

Cardinal Rimme, how did you know about Mr. Bootie?

Oh! Huh, Mr. Bootie is an old acquaintance of ours. (Rimme smiles).

Okay. Huh! You never cease to amaze me Cardinal. So let me guess. You set the whole thing up between me and Bootie to ship the American Sissy Baby, the **ASB**® [4.D-G8.2] to Africa?

Huh! Let's put it this way Mary. We'll always be there providing needed guidance. Kisss... And I'm sure the negotiation went well. Mr. Bootie, although human and not a very religious man, has a **Power-Shaft** [24.D] equivalent to a Cockolic Cardinal. And in fact, most men in Africa have a Power-Shaft.

Wow! So you orchestrated the whole thing? Cool! And here I was thinking I pulled off the deal of the century with Jamitin. But hey! Haa ha... I ain't complaining. I definitely want more Black lovers!

Well good. And Mary, in the future you will not need Yaoi and I to help you with your profiteering. You're very gifted at riding Shafts. And this is why we had you spent the last four years of college practicing on mine. Shaft manipulation is necessary in this Alpha Stud male dominated world.

Thank you! Mwah... (Mary embraces Rimme for a goodbye hug). Sniff... Snifff... I'll miss you. Mwah...

Yaoi and I love you Gurls sooo very much. (Rimme holds Mary tight). And don't worry. Cardinal **Jackeroff** will fill you when needed. Okay?

Okay. Snifff.... Mwah...

Well we're off. Have a pleasant journey to Africa! Mwah... See you soon.

[3.4] ROAD TRIP

Shoving off to Africa...

Honey did you pack the butt-plugs?

Yes Dear! You know I want you to save every morsel of Sissy-Poop® and Sissygasm goop for me.

Good! And **Jane**, you know I want you to stay close to me?

Haa… haa… Yeah I'll be right by your side the whole time. Geeezzz… **Mary** you're paranoid about this trip!

No, I'm not! Well kinda. I just never been to Africa or for that matter, hell I've never been outside of the USA Inc.

Ahhh…**Mare**, why are we going again?

Jane we're going on the road to meet with our network. This is going to be a really important trip to build confidence in the POOP program.

Oooh! Oh, I always pop a load whenever you say the word poop! Ahh… Whoops! And I pooped my panties!

Oh Jane you're going to have to change them a lot on this trip, we have a Cardinal Pimp, four President's and seven CI Grand Masters to visit in just three weeks. Remember Jane, STAY CLOSE!

[3.5] AFRICA

The Gurls land on the African continent…

Wow! **Jane** it's kinda warm here!

Yeah **Mare**, I'm glad I'm not wearing much.

Jane, you never wear much! (Jane is only wearing a skirtini and a halter top and six inch pumps).

True, but I'm ready for action! I keep thinking about what Rimme told you about Power-Shafts! I seriously want Black-Shafts up my Sissy cooch.

Jane! Just stay close please. (The Gurls step out of the jet and see Jamitin waiting).

Ahh! Ms. **Dune**! Jane, how was the trip? (Jamitin greets the Gurls).

Long but pleasant! **Jamitin**, but it was a nice flight, Jane entertained and I got some work done on my laptop.

Great, great… Let's get into the limo and cool off.

Wow, thanks for meeting us at the airport **Jamitin**.

My pleasure **Mary**! Ummm… Kiss… Ahhhh… I missed you. Kissss… Mwah…

I missed your big black boner Jamitin and you my Lover. (Mary runs her hands over his chest). Mwah…

Oh and Jane, you little Nymph, how are you my sweet little Gurl? Mwah…

Good now that I have you to play with! Haa haaa... Mwah…

Oh Jane Ahhhh! That feels sooo good. (Jane's stroking his huge boner). Yeah…

It was quite a trip. The flight crew of 6 females and 9 male passengers which were my play toys on the flight.

Oh Jane! Agh! You are an opportunist! Mwah…

Yep! And now I'm your new toy. Mwah…

Ahhhh… Mary! Kiss, Kiss.... (Mary, Jane & Jamitin caressing in the back seat of the limo) Hmmm...

But Jamitin your wife? Are you sure this is okay with her?

Oh! Please, we're a very modern family. Mary, did you know we privately practice Cockolicism.

Wow! That is a little progressive for an African family!

Yes, well we're a professional couple with a broader prospective. I mean, Africa has never been closely tied to Catholicism or Islam for that matter. It's not really a religious continent overall. Sexually wise it's been more of a, screw anything, anytime, type of culture, religion just gets in the way of good times and promiscuity.

Okay, well Jamitin, than I think we're going to work really well together. As sissies, Jane and I practice a **Bonobo-Way** [22.19] lifestyle.

Yes Mary, this is a union made in heaven. I feel we'll be working together for many, many years, prosperity is our destiny! And don't forget the **Bonobo** monkey originated here on the African continent.

Jamitin, I look forward to our ventures. We're on the precipice of making changes to sexual and monetary systems of society.

I agree Mary. Tell me. Have you ever heard about the global orgasmization called the Cock-Illuminati, the **CI?** [23.16.2].

Haa haaa! Yes Jamitin, I know many things about this secretive group. Jane and I have even had encounters with them, very intimate encounters? (Mary doesn't divulge her position as a Pimped-Nun in the Cockolic church).

Ahhhh… Do tell? Hmmm… It sounds very juicy!

Jamitin, let's just say, Jane and I have taken them. I mean our affiliation with the NSA and HCC has compelled us into engaging with men of great stature in society and government. And this of course led to sensuous situations.

I see! Coitus would qualify as a sensuous situation?

Haahaa… Yes Jamitin. Jane and I deal with this CI group on all levels. And it's a very aggressive group of well-endowed men, business and sexually speaking.

Mary, I have to confess something to you. I'm a member of the Cock-Illuminati.

Wow! Jamitin you're in the CI? Well that would explain you having a **Power-Shaft**® [24.D].

Yes, I'm in the CI African group, the CIA.

Okay! I see how you could be involved with them. You're very successful at business, politics and sexually, all the makings of a Grand Master.

Are you? Are you a Grand Master?

Yes Mary, I'm a level 6, degree 9, Grandmaster. I'm the Supreme Leader, first in command here on the African Continent.

Well Jamitin, then I have to assume you know the HCC agenda here in Africa?

Yes, yes Mary I know, the CI have all sworn an oath to the HCC and the Religious Union Brotherhood, the **RUB** [21.B.24.1].

Wow! Okay, so we're all on the same page?

Oh certainly! Mary, there's nothing to hid here, I'm the one you'll depend on to infect this entire continent! I assure you. Sissydom® will spread like wildfire.

Why here Jamitin? Why will it grow fast here?

Oh Mary, like I was saying, Africa has never bought into the European Catholicism or religious fever of Islam. We're a peaceful, horny group of people who enjoys life and the pleasures it provides us. Humans have been screwing animals in the ass forever! The cross-bred Bonobo creatures will bring great joy to us!

Okay, I see where you're going here. The South Americans the Europeans are a religious culture, the Asians are a philosophical group based on peace, harmony and tradition. Yeah, this is probably the only place on earth where the American beachhead can be established.

Yes, and also, there are many African-Americans who repatriated to Africa after the US lost the Financial World War, the **FWW** [23.24]. This was known as the **Great Exodus** [23.55] from the failing US money-hegemony system.

Right, right… Well Jamitin, so you think we have a good shot here in Africa because of the large African-American immigrants?

Yes, yes… Sissydom will have a very good shot here. I promise you this Mary! It will spread like a fever, there will be an American Sissy baby impaled on every African hardon within six point nine years!

[3.6] SEEDS

Production discussed…

Tomorrow we'll deliver the first orphaned babies we brought with us. We only have six babies as a token of our commitment to the implementation of the program. And there's another nine on the way.

Great, great… Well, we have many families who are just overwhelmed by the opportunity to own, I mean adopt an American pet.

Jamitin, you mean baby?

Yes, yes… Excuse me. American babies. This will be a momentous occasion for the African Union nations and the USA Inc. Mary, can I trust you?

What do you mean Jamitin? Of course you can! Mwah… We've shared our bodies so I assume we can share openly.

Mwah… Yes, but will you be able to keep up with the demand? Let's face it. The **Vaganus**® is the only product the USA Inc. produces. It's not an exporting Cunt-trie anymore.

Jamitin, we have the babies raised at farms. They're Farm Breed Sissy, **FBS**® [1.A2.6]. And the breeding farms are huge! We produce six thousand nine hundred Sissy babies every 69 days! We'll deliver, don't worry.

Okay, I'm glad to hear this, because once we start the infection process it will be like the plague. A sexual plague! Everyone will want to fuck a Vaganus®! And now I'm aroused. Mwah…

Ahhh… Jam-It-In my African lover! Agh! Kiss… Yes, pull it out of Jane and screw me! Aghhh… Kisss… Mwah…

[3.7] FAMILY

The Bootie family home…

Hello and well cum, Kiss, kissss….

Hi **Mrs. Bootee** I'm **Mary** this is **Jane** my wife.

Oooh! It is sooo good to finally meet you both. Jamitin has told me so much about you. Mwah…

Same here. Jamitin has shared photos and stories we us. We're also happy to meet you and have this opportunity to visit. And Africa is so fascinating! Ahhh… It's beautiful here!

Yes, yes… Mwah… Mwah… You will see and experience truly wonderful places and things here! (Mrs. Bootee undoes her blouse and wraps her arms around Mary, squeezing her ass and tits). Mwah…

Oooh! Hmmm... Kiss, kisss... Hmmm... Yes, this is going to be a wonderful experience, Kiss... Mrs. Bootee! Mwah…

Mwah… Please call me Sarah. Mwah…

Oh Sarah, Uoooh... I just got a little dizzy, I think I need to lay down for a bit and deal with this jetlag. Mwah…

Mwah… Sure, this is yours and Jane's room. Kisss... Let us know if you need.... (Mary interrupts).

Ummm… I need you to lay down with me Sarah? Please... (Mary is hugging Sarah, feeling her up). Mwah…

Oooh! My dear! How I've longed to be with you Mary. The stories Jamitin has told me about you and Jane. Ahhh… Kiss, Ummm... (Mary & Sarah are locked in an embrace on the bed).

Ahhh… Hello Jane. Mwah… Hey let's all have some Girl-on-Gurl time. Ummmm.... Kissss… Oooh Mary, Jane, you both look and feel as beautiful as Jamitin described you!

And you too Sarah. Jamitin has sent us some revealing photos of you. It's not much but my clit is fully erect for you (Mary whispers in Sarah's ear). Do you want me Sarah?

Oooh! I've dreamed of making love with Sissies… Hmmm… Kisss… You're my first Gurls I've ever made love to. Mwah… Oooh… Now I know why men be cum ad-Dick-ted to you. Huh! Ummm… Yeah…. (Sarah is panting in-heat for Sissy-Sex).

[3.8] BABIES

Here we are the first home. Ahhh… Look at the parents they're so glad to see us! Hello! (Jamitin shout from the window of the car).

Yes, everything looks nice, a very well kept place, flower beds, nice lawn and luxury cars, beautiful neighborhood, very sweet. (Mary is impressed with the up-scale of the place). It looks nicer than the house I grow up in.

Hello! Well cum to our home. I'm **Develan** and this is my husband **Lucifer**.

Hi I'm Ms. Dune this is Jane my assistant.

Well cum and this is the baby? Ahhh... Sooo beautiful (Mary passes the baby to the adopting mother).

Yes she is adorable. Have you chosen a name yet?

Yes, we're going to call her Trap.

Huh! Ahhh... It's a very unique name!

Yes, we feel it will suite her well in our modern society. I mean with all the new sexually liberated ways children are raised these days.

Yes and very different. Slightly on the slutty side, but like you said, very appropriate for a young girl not involved in the Whoring industry. (Mary tries to swerve her way around the situation).

Pssss... Jamitin! (Mary pulls Jamitin to the side) Ahhh... Trap, not really an appropriate name for a girl if you know what I mean? For Sissy maybe but not for a human kid!

Ahhhh... Mary cum here for a moment. No secretes between us. Look, I wasn't very transparent with you before. The parents know!

Know what? (Mary has a shocked look on her face).

The adopting families know the American orphan babies are Sissies.

Jizz-Us... !!!...

Jamitin! Man! (Mary is really furious). Okay! Well, I have no idea if you can even get away with this in Africa, but in the USA Inc. it's called fraud. And it's only legal if the government does it. This is disappointing. Huh! (Mary sighs).

No worries Mary! Fraud is a way of life here! Look, the families know the babies are **ASB** and they're happy. Oh and by the way, these families we're visiting today are all in the Cock-Illuminati Africa, the **CIA** [23.16.2].

What! They're all **CI** families! You didn't tell me they were gonna be CI!

Yeah, I know I should have told you Mary, but we can't take the chance of anything going wrong with this first batch. It was too risky to divulge our plans back in Washingcum. Are you mad at me Mary? Mwah...

Okay, okay... Huh! Jamitin, no I'm not mad at you. Mwah... I mean, I've never been to Africa. Heck! You're the only Black lover I've ever had. You know what's happening here sexually speaking. Just tell me the plan.

Thanks Mary. Mwah... I knew you'd understand. I will give you the full length of my appreciation tonight in bed. Kiss. But for now, just play along with my infection plan.

Wah... Wah... Wah... (Baby crying for nutriment). Oooh! I'm your new Momma, Ahh... She's happy! Uoooh, she went straight for my tit. Wow!

And Develan, these are the cases of baby formula.

Oooh great! The folks at the POOP® office told me it's a special formula and how we must use only the formula supplied to us from America.

Yes, yes… This is a very special baby formula (Actually bottled sperm for Sissies).

Well here Honey, let me and the boys manage the baby and the formula while you and Mary go chat about the program.

Oooh Lucifer! Darling, Kiss... You're so sweet. Mwah…

Jane Honey! Can you stay with the guys and help with the feeding?

Ahhh… Sure Boss, you know you don't have to force me to hang-out with big strong men. See yah. (Jane happily is hanging all over Lucifer and his sons).

Oh your husband is so nice! Big guy too! He looks very strong. Hmmm… (Mary licks her lips checking-out the buff husband).

Yeah! Lucifer is a big man.

And your four boys are all so big and handsome as well.

Oh my sons? Yes, they're growing like weeds and big like their Daddy in every way. (Develan gives a knowing wink and smile at Mary). Mwah…

Develan!

Don't be coy with me Mary. Mwah… We're both Ladies. Cum! Cum into my boudoir. We need Gurl-on-Girl time. Mwah…

Huh! You know I'm a Gurl?

[3.9] FEEDING

Here you go little one. Hmmm… Yes you are hungry! My, my... It's just as **Jamitin** told me it would be. You're hungry for Man-Cream® you Sissy nympho. Yes you are. Yes you are.

Dad, Dad… Can we feed the baby too? You know, not from the bottle, form you know?

Well… Hmmm… (Dad contemplates the situation).

Pleeeease…. Dad! Pleeeease…. (The boys are all restlessly massaging their young feeding hoses still yearning to be freed from their shorts).

Okay, but let me show you how first. Look here in the Sissydom manual at the Sissy Feeding **Procedure** [4.D-G2.5] instructions.

Sure Dad! I'll read it. Procedure: the erect penis (feeding hose) at no time may enter the throat of the animal. Therefore only the tip (cockhead) may enter the mouth of the Sissy.

Right! Okay boys. Watch how carefully I insert my hose. Ooooh, yeah! Okay suckle on your new Daddy my little white princess, Ooooh!

Oh! Wow! Dad she's sucking on you! Oh man! This is cool! (The boys are all naked with erects in hand, anxiously waiting their turn).

Yes, you don't have to force it down their throats. Remember just make it available to them. Oh! Hi Jane, what a surprise! Wow! You wanna help us stay hard? (Jane's on her knees fluffing the boys).

Oh don't mind me Lucifer. I just love watching well hung men like you and your boys being maternal. Do you mind?

What, what are doing Jane?

Oooh! Nice Cocks! I'm just as hungry as the baby. Hmmm... Guk... Gak... Gek.... Big Black Boners! Kiss... (Jane kisses the tip of the dad's huge hardon) Agh! (Jane easily takes Lucifer's entire Power-Shaft and the boys watch on attentively wanting to be next).

Jerome! Son, get in here are feed the baby, while Jane here performs her, Snake-Swallowing, circus trick on my manhood.

I'm next, I'm next! Wow! She swallowed the whole thing Dad! Whoa! That's amazing!

Several deliveries later...

Okay all the babies are delivered! Whooohooo... It was a great day for the POOP®.

Yes, yes... It was and very interesting to check-out the adoption families. I'd say everything went well?

Oh yeah! I think these first families will do great and it's a good thing they fully realize what they're getting into. I agree Jamitin. It was a good call about setting them up with CI families.

Right Mary. And I know the baby formula is sufficient for the children but the CI families will be able to feed fresh sperm to the babies who will give them a healthier environment, nutrition-wise and emotionally. Especially seeing how most of the families have four or more sons.

Yeah, I'm all for it Jamitin. Having grown up in a fully Sissified® family I realize the children will have a normal upbringing. Especially considering the babies are all **Bitch®** Sissies. They'll need every drop of sperm they can drain out of the males available to them.

[3.10] TRAINING

Instruction manual distribution…

So **Jamitin**, what's going to happen when we need to distribute the babies to normal non-CI African families?

Oh, we got this covered Mary. The CI families will be the support team. They'll train and educate the normal folks into feeding the child in a more intimate way. We adapted the American National Sissy Training Program, the **NSTP** [4.D-G1.30].

Wow! Jamitin. You're awesome dude! Mwah…

Mwah… Yep! And also the Sissy Sexual Trainers, the **SST** [4.D-G3.1], and the Sissy Family Support Program, the **SFSP** [4.D-G2.4]. Here in Africa we're all onboard with the programs you established in the United States Inc. We're going to strictly adhere to the Official Sissydom Manual, the SM069.

Cool Jamitin. This is more than I expected! And I feel because the babies are all **Bitch®** types which have the highest Cockage scores, there'll be even more Africans infected with the Sissy **Pheromones** [18.13a].

Yes Mary, I feel the same, we'll have an increased spread of infection without the **DOM**® types. Here the Human females can assume the role of the DOM and be the Bitches trainer and Mistress. We'll just supply collars and leashes to the human females. Mary we'll have total control of these Bitches!

Wait, wait, wait… What are you saying Jamitin? Collars and leashes? You mean you're going to treat the Sissies like pets not as humans? This is not how we do it back in the USA Inc! Are we gonna re-educate the families into accepting an African version of Sissydom®, with no Sissy Rights regulations?

Mary, relax! (Jamitin puts his arm around Mary). Look, do you really understand what's actually happening here? I mean with the adoption program?

Huh! I think you weren't completely honest with me, Jamitin. Every time I ask a specific questions about your African program you slip your long Black snake of cock up in my lovehole and then. Yeah huh! I'm having so many orgasms, I stop knowing what-the-fuck is going on.

Oh Mary! Mwah… Here let me slip it in again, you Sissies think more clearly when there is a man in your Vaganus. (Jamitin reaches into his shorts and pulls out his long appendage then twirls it around for Mary).

[3.11] REVERSAL

Soft Black-Supremacy (SBS) discussed…

NO! Jamitin! Please inform me of everything. We'll play later. (Mary's kinda turned off by Jamitin not being forthcoming about the information). I have no idea what the hell you're up to Jamitin! And it's making me uneasy.

Okay, okay... Mary, I'll tell you the real deal here. Look, we have all these African families adopting white American babies. Do you know what this means from a cultural point of view?

Clueless!

Mary it means these families are breeding into the white world. They're integrating into Whitey's world!

Tsss... What are you talking about?

They love this kind of thing. Africans enjoy associating the white folks! And through adoption at least part of their family will be white. Do you see what I'm saying? The white child is a trophy of conquest!

You lost me there!

Hmmm... Think of zebras! You have black and white.

Ahhh! Yeah I guess. But, big deal! Africans nowadays are wealthier and more educated than the Caucasians back in the USA Inc. What conquest are we even talking about? And why deprecate downward? Why not trade-up away from Caucasians? Sorry I don't get this.

Because Mary it's very fashionable to have a Whitey in the house, it's like having a better car, or if your lawn looks greener than your neighbors. It's a status symbol.

Okay, I follow you. Then you're saying its prestigious to have a White baby?

Yeah! Now you get it, Mary! So, if the African males in the family have to dispense man-milk into the white American Sissy mouth with their cum-hoses, this is fine and acceptable! This is a total flip flop of history.

What do you mean, flip flop?

Master-Slave. Whitey-Master, Black-Slave and now it's Black-Master, White-Slave. Mary, something's about your American history will never be forgotten. At least not in Africa or by African-Americans.

So, you're saying it's a total reversal?

Yes, yes... I can see in the not too distant future an adopted white American Sissy daughter walking down the street with a collar around her neck being led on a leash by her Black African father.

Wow! Jamitin, you sure you want Africa to turn out like that?

Sure, sure! And even to the point where it would be acceptable for the Caucasian American Sissy daughter to perform fellatio on her African father in public as a sign of humility of the white race! People here would applaud stuff like this! It's called cultural pay-back.

Well sure Jamitin. After the middle working class in the USA Inc. was eradicated or confined to FEMA camps, the USA Inc. government invented a Whoring animal, the Sissy. I mean Americans applaud public demonstrations of Sissy loyalty. The POM, FO, PBJ are all to humiliate the Sissy in public. It's very common for the wealthy bourgeoisie in the States to spit, piss and ejaculate onto Sissies. But it has all been legalized and has no racial meaning associated with it.

Mary change is cuming to the African continent. There is talk about the Soft Black-Supremacy, the **SBS** [22.29] movement.

Soft Black what? Are you crazy? Supremacy is discrimination!

No Mary, just the opposite. Whitey is too stupid to be in control of anything. The Caucasians are like animals, they need to be controlled.

Wow! This is a little freaky, a reverse roll discrimination?

SBS (Soft Black-Supremacy) the law would be passed by the African Union (AU) to create a new social-class of White Race (including Caucasian) human folks who may temporarily reside on the African continent. (1) All Whitey people will be assigned and work for a Black Master. (2) Whitey will obey Master. (3) Whitey can be deported at any time. (4) Whitey (man or women) will bend-over when told to and be paid for labor with sex from the Master. (5) Whitey will not be physically injured. (6) Whitey may not own anything. (6) Whitey is taxed for their earned in cum as are the American working class.

Okay! This all sounds good to me! I'm a Sissy, screw the violent greed humans! Huh! More Sperm for me!

Yes Jane, you understand me! Good Gurl! (Jamitin embraces Jane). Mwah… Anything to do with sperm sounds good to you. Kiss.... Kissss... kisss....

Honey what have you been up to? (Mary asks).

Ahh nothing! Playing with the boys.

Hah! Right Jane, you have Jizzies all over your face. Mwah…

Jamitin, I'm with you dude. It sounds less Bonobo than I was expecting but hey! Africa will benefit from **Sissy-Sex** [15-69.7] regardless of how many White slaves you have.

Departure at the airport…

Hey mission accomplished Jamitin. We did good. Look, I just don't want the Sissies abused.

Don't worry Mary. Mwah… Everything is fine. I'm sorry I scared you with the Black Supremacy stuff. Mwah…

Okay, okay… I trust you Jamitin. So, off to the next destination. Istanbul!

Well, good luck to you both. And Mary, all this is about domination through ad-Dick-tion. Mwah…

> ### *World Cock domination*
> ### *through, Vaganus ad-dick-tion*

Mwah… Yeah Jamitin, we'll discuss this later, I'm really not happy about the Sissies being handle like pets. Mwah…

Mary it would be an issue if the Sissies were DOM types like you, but the babies are all B-Type! And the Bitches like the abuse. Don't worry they'll be fine and well cared for. We have plenty of veterinarians and kennels in Africa. Goodbye my friend! Kiss… Mwah… Mwah… Goodbye Mwah…

Chapter 4: Networking

[4.1] ROAD TRIP

Mare hey! How cum we can't just go to Rome and visit with the Holy-Cock? I mean the Pope?

Because **Jane** we're taking care of POOP business Sweetheart.

I don't get any say in this do I?

Mwah... Ooooh my little pouty Sweetheart we'll visit Rome someday but, we got work to do. Kisss... Umm.... Cum here! (Mary gives Jane a motherly hug). You're so cute. Mwah...

Really, what are we doing in a place like **Turkey**?

Turkey is nice place! The Byzantine Empire, Constantinople, ancient history. We're here so we can meet with the Russians. You see we can't go to Russia because both Cunt-tries still have sanctions against each other.

Okay, they have always had sanctions and it's totally ridiculous because those things only work if your allies follow the sanctions with you. And the USA Inc. has no allies since its adaption of Sissydom, its denouncement of democracy, withdrawal from the Climate and Climax accords.

Right! The USA Inc. turned into the failing empire that doesn't play well with others. Let a spoiled kid in a playground. So anyway! We're here on a very important mission. We're gonna meet, I mean pursued the Cardinal from the Russian Orthodox HCC and the Cock-Illuminati representatives to play with us.

Great! Good news. We'll be meeting up and taking it up our Gurl-Pussies as a sign of good diplomacy!

Yeah, yeah… Haa haaa… Ooh Jane! It's always about the Coochee with you. Cume here! Kiss. **Istanbul** here we cum!

[4.2] RUSSIAN CONNECTION

My Excellency! (The Gurls go down on one knee and kiss the Cardinal on her holy ordained cockhead).

Ahhhh… Ms. Dune, how are you?

Good, very good Cardinal **Popoff**. (The Gurls are in a trance gaping at the erect Holy penis on display). The trip was great. And Istanbul is fascinating.

Great! I'm so glad you're here, I've heard so much about you and Jane your Bitch wife. And Cardinal **Rimme** asked me to treat you particularly well.

Yes, I'm her branded Harem Whore® so she's very interested in what transpires here.

Yes! And having met you I can see why. You're quite attractive Mary. Mwah… Rimme tells me you're his favorite. Hmmm… (The Cardinal is slobbering all over Mary's neckline and feeling her up like a kid on his first date).

Soooo! (Mary gently nudges her away). Cardinal **Popoff** I'm excited about the potential of our meeting and the introduction of the **MSES** [23.13] into Russia.

Sheeesh... Not too loud Mary. (The Cardinal whispers). This is Istanbul, there're spies here as there have been for centuries. Yes

I agree. The proposal Cardinal Rimme informed me about is intriguing. We could profit handsomely from this scheme.

Absolutely Cardinal. This arrangement, I know you'll agree, has benefits for all parties!

Well yes! On the surface it looks like a well thought out scheme to dominate the penetration-hole market. But Ms. Dune.

Please your Holiness, call me Mary.

Sure Sister Mary. This is what we see when we look at the POOP plan strategy. We get free American Sissy Babies, the **ASB**® [4.D-G3.12] you get the labor compensation transaction plan implemented, the **LCT**® [4.D-G2.27]. This is more or less like the SWIFT system of years gone by?

Right Cardinal **Popoff**. We provide all the Sissy **Vaganus**® [14.O1.6] you need as we have done in the past with the US dollars and we get a small gratuity for the service of course. Call it, sex hegemony.

Yes, as far as the Orthodox **HCC**® [9] sect of the Church in Russia is concerned, we're fine with the American deal. It's the Cock-Illuminati, the RU-CI group who I'm concerned about and their portion of the profit.

Yes, yes! But this is fine! There's an additional fee built into the **LCT** charge. We have no problem with compensating the Russian **CI** [9.I4.4] group for supporting the program. The USA Inc. has always given gratuities to its affiliated Mafia and Fascist groups throughout history. So Cardinal Popoff, when do we start shipping the babies?

Wow! Slow down Mary. Hmm... Rimme has taught you well, you're sharp, quick witted and beautiful. I have a hardon, I mean a hard copy document here for your **Signagasms** (Signatures in the year 2254 are made with the Jizzed tip of a Cock or Sissy Cocklette). Then I'll WeeChat a digital copy to you, Rimme and the Holy-Pope in Rome.

Great Cardinal! And I'm hungry and I'm sure Jane is by now. So where can we perform the Strategy Agreement Consummation, the **SAC** [22.24] and sign the documents?

Well the best cumference rooms and restaurant in Istanbul is right down the street. They have this dish which isn't on the menu. An imported American Sissy-Poop® dish to die for!

Okay sure! But first, I need a quick liquid lunch Cum-Union from your Holy nut sack (Mary gets on her knees with her mouth wide open). Gak... Guk... (Several minutes later). Ummm.... Thanks for Popping off Cardinal. Hee heee pun intended. Heee... hee.... Yummy, you were delicious. Mwah...

Thank you my dear. Mwah... So maybe we should get going for lunch and then the cumference room?

Sure! Let me find Jane. Jane. She was here? (Mary looks around and has no sight of Jane). Jane. Hey Jane! Ahhh... (Mary has a frantic look on her face). Oh Poop! JANE! Where'd she go?

I don't know! (Popoff replies). She is not with the bodyguards!

Jane! Jane! Shoot! I'll call her cell. Beep, beep, beep.... She's not answering. Tssss... Dang-it! Jane pickup! Beep, beep, beep.... Un-fuck-believable! I told her to stay close! Jane! (Mary is shouting her lovers name in desperation of finding her). Jane!

Mary! Something's going on here. There's a crowd gathering over there. Here's the CI representative, I'll see what's going on.

Yes, yes... Okay, (Popoff is talking to the CI guys). Right, right, okay. What can we do? I see. Right, okay keep me informed. Mary! I'm sorry, Jane's not here.

Oooh Fuck! I told her to stay close!

Ahhh**hhh**...!!!...

Mary, the CI guys think she was taken by some Middle-Eastern looking guys when she was shopping in the bazar. They spotted her near a dildo vendor's cart.

Holy-Poop Shit! Where the-fuck is she?

We'll find her. Don't worry. Calm down Mary. They couldn't have gone far.

Jane! I can't lose her Popoff. Sniff... Snifff... Huh! (Mary cries at the thought of losing her lifelong companion).

Three days later....

[4.3] EXTRACTION

Chuf, chuf, chuf.... (Helicopter sound) JANE! JUMP! JUMP NOW!

Chuf, chuf, chuf.... (Jane jumps and the airmen pull her into the chopper).

Okay, you're in! Hold on! Where did you go? (Mary shouts over the loud noise of the helicopter).

I didn't go anywhere! I was staying close like we agreed!

Well what-the-fuck happened?

I was taken by these Muslim dudes!

Did they hurt you?

NO! NO! I just had the best fucking three days of my life..!!!... (Being weak from her adventure, Jane tries to shout but can't very well).

Chuf, chuf, chuf...

What? I can't hear you! It's too loud in the helicopter, put these headphones on we can talk on the radios!

Chuf, chuf, chuf.... (Loud helicopter noise).

Okay, that's better. We don't have to shout now. What did you say? You had three days of yuck?

Huh! No! Mare, I said I had three glorious-fuck-days of fuck!

Great! Snifff... **Jane**, I thought I lost you, (The Gurls do a reuniting hug) Sniff, sniff, (Mary cries out of fear of losing Jane). I don't think I handle losing you Jane. Snifff... (Mary vises Jane's head between her hands and says sternly while staring into her eyes). Don't you ever leave me again! Sniff... Sniff...

Mare! I told you I didn't leave you, I was taken. I wondered over to the street cart selling these really cool looking double-ended dildos. I just wanted a souvenir from Istanbul. And I thought I was fine, I could see the security guards watching me.

Jane! Who took you?

I told you a big gang of Muslims. These real handsome Middle-Eastern dudes surrounded me.

How Jane? If you could see the security guards and they could see you? How did you just suddenly go missing?

Ahhh... I remember I picked out this really exotic looking dildo. And then the dude said if I wanted try it before purchase, he had a little bed-mat in the cart. So I was like, yeah why not!

Jane! So you just what? Slipped into this stranger little vending cart? What were you thinking? (Mary is freaking out).

Yeah! Mare, I just wanted to give it a try and by then I was super freaken horny! So I figured, yeah! Why not. I went inside his tiny little cart and I slipped one head in my cunt, then laid down with my legs over my head and put the free end in my mouth.

Pssss... Jane! I really do need to put a leash on you. You have no sense of danger, or awareness of a possible threat! Huh! I can't leave you alone!

Well look! They were nice people. The next thing I know, I was in some palace somewhere.

They must have had a Teleportation device in the cart?

I guess. But Mare. I wasn't in danger. Hell if they hadn't switched my cell phone back on and put it in my purse you wouldn't have gotten my GPS location. And Mary, they treated me like a goddess! Like I said. I spent the last three days and nights being made love to. It was like being with our Pimps but multiplied.

How many men Jane?

I lost track! There were only about six guys who abducted me. And once we got to there, to this palace, the guys from the dildo cart were all there sharing me. And it was a really fancy place.

How many of them used my Gurl, Jane?

Whoa! Mare, it was cool! There were maybe, hundreds of them. Big, muscular, handsome, hairy, erotic looking men. It was heaven. I was pampered every moment.

Nobody screws my Gurl! Jane.

So, why you? I mean, aren't there women in Arabia with your make and model? Why take you? Ahh... Wait, I don't think women here have my Cockage® score!

True! Whores are probably in short supply!

But I'm sure there are tiny little promiscuous women like you around.

Hey I don't know Mare. All I know is, we went to this place called Mecca. And I had fun!

Yeah Mecca, it's where we extracted you from. So they had at you? I mean, what did they do to you?

Okay and we did this thing called the **Hajj** (EN09). It was wild! This really huge big guy was carrying me on his back and then he swung me around to his front, lifted up my robe and he inserted his manhood into me up to my belly! The robes covered everything so I think the other pilgrims around us just thought it was a father carrying his young crippled little daughter.

Tssss… Wonderful!

Oooh fuck Mare! I came so many times impaled on him as we walked seven freaken times around this weird looking square black building in the middle they called the Kaaba. Then we went to the palace and the ritual began on me. I was in and out of consciousness so I knew I was in a Fucked-Out. I didn't mind because by that time I knew these guys were cool. And awesome lovers! God-of-Cocks, I would go back every year and do it again. It was fantastic!

Yeah, really cool, Jane, I'm just glad you're not hurt. Did they ask you questions?

Yeah, yeah… They wanted to know what you did in Africa and what you were doing in Turkey with the Russians.

Okay! Now this is all clear to me. They wanted information out of you! Dam It! They were spying on us!

Hey I didn't tell them anything.

Jane, how do you know what you said, you told me you were in and out of consciousness you could have told them everything!

You got a point. I was having these orgasmic convolutions. During which they could have found out what my favorite drink at Studbucks® is, a Sissy **Frapa-Poopo-Cino**! Or that we're both

NUNS! Or I'm a Branded Whore. Wait. They could have just looked at the brand on my ass and figure that out! Mare! You're paranoid.

Right Jane so you think this is what they were fishing for non-pertinent information! This is really bad news.

Well I do remember babbling about Jamitin's enormous cock. I mean, what Gurl wouldn't? Geeez… What are you worried about Mare? You know the POOP plan is gonna work! You're going to **Sissify**® the entire world Babe. I believe in you, nothing is gonna stop this from happening! Besides, information? Nah! After three days of being bounced up and down on their poles, I think they were only interested in my hot Sissy ass!

Well yeah, I guess. Dam it! Now we have to tell Jamitin and Rimme these guys know about the African ad-Dick-tion deal. Oh Jane. I'm just glad you're okay.

Sorry Boss. Kiss… Mwah…

Ooh well, we just have to have faith the Sissy **Pheromones** [18.13a] emitted from the Vaganus® is more powerful than the vagina.

What do you mean?

I mean, once the ad-Dick-tion kicks in, like it had for the US dollar as the world's reserve currency, then we'll dominate by the will of the Cock. Men aren't so powerful when their balls are empty. They might rattle their swords and beat their chests but it's the Sissy-Puss that wins over the Cock. In our case we're the pussy replacement. The patented American Vaganus® is the new pussy. Hmmm... Mwah…

Ooh Boss! Mwah… I love how you can make a disaster sound like a win, win. Hmmm... Mwah…

Kisss...kiss... Let's get you back to the hotel and get some rest, we have to hit the road again tomorrow for Arizona. Hmm... Mwah…

[4.4] FARM

Phoenix Arizona. Wow! I thought Riyadh **Saudi Arabia** was hot! Jizz-Us! What a sweatbox this place is!

Well regardless, we gotta make it a quick inspection then we're back on the plane for Latin America. We gotta meet-up with our Cockolic Church Missionary Moms tonight.

Huh! In a million years I wouldn't have thought, one, our Mothers would both be Nuns and two, they're both on a mission to save the almighty Cockolic Church! I mean! Haa haaa…. What-the-fuck! This wasn't in the Sissy Family-Planning brochures!

Yeah our Moms are hot & horny Nuns in mini-skirts! Go figure!

At the Sissy Breeding Farm…

Ahhh… Director **Dune**! (The Senator agrees the Gurls on the Heliport pad).

Hey **Senator Humpme**!

You Gurls ready for this? (The Senator says as he grabs Mary's ass). Kisss… You are a real sugar pie Dune. Yeah… Hmmm… (Humpme is humping Mary like he's never had pussy in his life).

Ahhh… Yeah! (Mary tries to ward off his groping). Geeeezz… No disrespect Senator but. Get the-fuck-off of me! Huh! Anyway, yes I was briefed on the facility and process. I'm a little apprehensive about the whole Vaganus Industrial Complex, the **VIC** [25.43].

Well Dune, you of all people should know why this is so necessary.

Huh? Maybe I do Senator. (Mary, not being a Neocon warmonger, knows opinions vary as to why Sissydom exists).

Director, you being a Sissy had a lot to do with your Cumfirmation approval. We needed someone in control who knows the Sissy business. I mean, cultural significance is secondary to profit!

Huh! Let's just see what's going on here and take it from there. And **Senator Humpme**, you don't have to be grabbing my ass during the entire inspection. I mean hey, I don't mind a pat on the ass, but seriously! Take your hand out of panties!

Ma'am, (The military staff salutes **Mary**). Yes okay, you don't have to salute me. Geeez..!!!..

Director, you're a First Lieutenant in the US Sissy Reserves, **USSR** [25.26.2]. And this is a military controlled facility. So they're saluting an officer.

Oh yeah! I forgot, sorry (Mary blows the **Sissy-Salute** [25.9c] double air-kiss, to the enlisted Soldiers). Mwah… Mwah…

Director it would be appropriate to salute back.

Sure okay. Mwah… Mwah… (Mary Salutes). Why don't they salute Jane?

Bitches can't be officers. Jane's just a sergeant, the highest enlisted rank.

Arnnn…. Arnnn… (The noise of the alarm for the sliding security doors).

The facility is completely underground. Okay we're through the main doors and in the airlock/scanner.

Wow! The security is insane here.

Oooh yeah! Nobody cums or goes from here without clearance.

Arnnn…. Arnnn…

Okay we're through the level 3 doors, four more levels to go.

Wow! Senator why did they put this facility in your State?

Well Arizona is one of the States with the largest number of FEMA Camps. The detainees are mostly from other States but we had the most room. This is where we send all the dreads of society! You might say our FEMA camps in the USA Inc. are like debt-forgiveness centers.

Like a Debt Jubilee? [23.38]

Yeah, yeah… Dune! When the middle working class in this great Cunt-trie of ours can't pay their debts, we just imprison them in FEMA labor camps. And Dune! Haa haaa…There is no Jubilee!

Arnnn…. Arnnn…

And besides, it's easier to control a large prison population when they're too dam hot to run anywhere! Haaaa haaa haa.... You know what I mean sweetheart? Kisss… I bet I can make you really hot in that little Vaganus of yours?

Yeah, okay Senator **Humpme**... (Mary pushes him away). Let's just get this over with you misogynistic jerk! (Mary knows this Politicians a real asshole, he keeps rubbing his hardon against her).

Arnnn.... Arnnn... (Annoying security noise from the sliding doors).

Level 7 (Computer generated voice blares).

You gotta a hell of a temper there, little Gurl. Okay Director, if you wanna turn back this is your last chance.

Nah! I wanna see this. (Mary has heard some horrific descriptions about the VIC, so she braces herself for what might be behind the doors).

Okay, don't say I didn't warn you little Gurl. This is the Breeding Farm! (Humpme flings the doors open).

Holy-Cock! What-the-Fuck! (The racks of cocoons are several football fields long and wide and quite few stories tall) There're thousands of them! (Host human women hooked to umbilical cords lifelessly floating in tube shaped columns! Mary's is in total shock).

Yes, tens of thousands actually. We plan to expand to a hundred thousand in six month's nine days. This is the largest USA Inc. Government project ever attempted. Bigger than the Manhattan Project, WII, Hoover dam, the Pivot-to-Asia, Trumpism, the moon landing and the conquest of Latin America and Canada combined. We're putting everything we got into this project. Nothing is going to stop global infiltration! There will be an American **Vaganus**® in every bed in the World by the year 2300!

Jizz-Us! We have achieved total insanity. Senator! You're not a Human. You're a MONSTER..!!!... (Mary's really upset).

Director, call it what you want Gurl, this is the United States Inc. gaining **sexual hegemony** as we had the **financial hegemony** many years ago. Director Dune, if you gotta a better idea, let's hear it! The Vaganus® is our new weapon!

So many **Jane**, so many, Sniff... Sniff. (Mary looks away and starts crying about the inhuman thought of the Breeding Farm). This isn't right! What have we be cum?

Mary, are these all Sissy breeding mothers in the cocoons?

Yes, Jane, they're kept alive by being hooked-up to an umbilical cord and are in an unconsciousness state. They won't remember any of this.

Who are they?

Mostly no-names. Just Jane Doe's, FEMA Camp dwelling, criminal, homeless, jobless, spouseless, hopeless human women.

Will they still be all those things after they give birth to the Sissy babies? (Jane says in a naive voice).

Huh! Yes Jane, Sniff, sniff... They will always be abused. Sniff, sniff... And the Sissies they give birth to will be nothing more than livestock animals. **FBS** kids. Used, treated and discarded as animals. Sniff, sniff, sniff, sniff... Let's just get out of here! (Mary runs for the doors they entered from).

What wrong Dune? (The Senator shouts in a diabolical satanic voice at Mary as she flees the horror of the space).

Yeah! I'm not feeling so good. You deranged son of bitch! (Mary shouts back in disgust for what she sees as her Cunt-tries falling into).

Wait for me Mare! (Jane follows Mary out).

Sniff... Sniff.... Sorry Jane. I gotta get out of here. (Mary's starting to understand the Human bureaucracy she deals with in the Washingcum is only concerned about profit not the welfare of anyone).

[4.5] LA

The Gurls land in Latin America…

Mom! **Heather**!

Mom! **Sandy**! (Mary shouts).

We love you so much, Kiss...Kisss... Mom! (Hugging reunion). Mwah… Mwah… Umm… I miss you both.

Ooooh **Mary**, **Jane**! Mwah… We miss you! Mwah…

We miss you sooo much! Mwah…

Cum on Mom, let's go to the hotel and get caught-up on what's going on here.

Yeah, the hotel's a safe place let's go.

Wait, a safe place?

Yes, Honey, you ain't in Sissydom® anymore! Latin America is a battlefield.

Wait! What are you talking about? I thought this was a peace mission? You guys are supposed to be down here converting Sissy-less souls over to Cockolicism?

Mary this place is Vagina Cunt tree! The urban areas are controlled by the **Contra-Vaganus®** [20.1] VAC Army. Americans are targets! They know we're here for one thing. To infiltrate their moral fabric which is all centered on Vagina worship. It's totally crazy! We're offering salvation through unlimited penetration of the Vaganus® and this macho culture thinks we're here to harm them!

Okay, okay, slow down and calm down Mom. We'll figure it all out in the morning.

In bed for the night…

Ahhh… Sandy the Gurls haven't changed! Aghhh!

Oh My Cock-God! Heather they still munch on our cunts like they did when they were little hungry Sissy babies! Aghhh!

Yeah! We raised them well! Aghhh! Kiss... Kisss... Mary Sweetheart, put it back in mommy. Ahhh… Mwah… Love you Sandy. (Heather is taking Mary's Cocklette while making-out with Sandy). Ahhh… Yeah, do mommy! Mwah…

Ahhhh... Girl, I Love you too Heather! (Their moms are making out and have been lovers since before the Gurls were born). Kiss… Kissss… Ummm…

Mom!

Mom! What are you guys lovers? Mwah…

Oooh! Mary, we've always been in love with each other!

So you guys are what? Lesbians.

Ahhh… Me and Sandy love each other, leave it at that. Mwah… We love each other, so what! Mwah…

Next Morning…

Hmmm… I loved waking up with you Gurls.

Ummm… Me too Mom. Mwah… You and Sandy are Super Moms. We love sleeping with you.

Oooh! Cum here! Haa haaa… Jane you love fisting mommy in the ass? Don't you? You are so precious! Mwah…

Ahh Mom you make me feel so good…

Hey Mary! Can you help me in the kitchen for a moment?

Mary and her mom Heather have private time…

Mary how's Jane been doing?

Oh! Well, let me see, she got kidnapped in the Middle-East! She made love with everyone we've met. You know. Typical Jane.

Okay, so this all sounds normal right? Hmm... This would account for that.

Mom! Account for what? What are you getting at? And why all these questions about Jane? Look! Jane's a lot a work, okay!

Do you love her?

Mom! Huh! of course I do! You know that. But? (Mary sighs and pauses). I'm a director of a government program now. I have a lot of people depending on me!

Honey, you know Jane will always be there for you. So, yeah, she's a hand full, she always has been. But she's your wife and you have a Sissy-Bond with her. You two are a registered Bonded Sissy Pair, a **BSP** [4.D-G3.7].

I know! And why are you reminding me? I love her and wouldn't think of spending a day without her. I think she's actually a little bit more responsible lately.

I hope so! After having you as her DOM, she should be.

Haaa... haa...Yeah you gotta point. She is calmer now and doesn't do some of the silly stuff she used to do, like staying out all night without me and she's more selective about who does an FO on her now. What did you say about account for something?

Oh! When you Gurls were over there in the Middle-East Jane's **Cockage**® spiked really high.

Huh! Yeah, that was my bad, Mom. I let her out of my sight for a while and she managed to get herself abducted by a gang of Arab dudes and ended up at the Hajj. And it's a long story. She's fine!

Well good, I'm glad she's not whoring around anymore and it's good to know you're so emotionally tied to her, because today we're going to use Jane as jailbait!

Mom! **Jailbait**? Cum-on. Don't fuck-around with me like that. Okay? The Middle-East was enough adventure for a while.

Yeah, you Mary, we have to draw the vagina loving males out of the jungle and trap them into enjoying Sissy-Puss. And in the case of Jane she has a HCC Holy Sanctified Vaganus® which makes perfect bait.

Okay Mom. I can't believe I'm hearing this. When you're done glorifying my wifes lovehole, tell me how this is going to attract the opposing guerilla forces out of the jungle? Not to mention, why, if they're vagina loving freaks, would they want anything to do with Jane the anti-vagina nymph?

Oh! Well that's silly Darling! Of course they're not just going to pop out of the jungle for Jane! I mean, she looks like a petite little sexy seven year old boy with long blonde hair. These guys are way too religious to wanna rape a little **Sissy-Gurl** like Jane.

Yeah! My point Mom!

Okay, so this is why Sandy and I are going to flaunt our vagina's, alluring the horny men out into the open.

No, No, No! No way! Are you and Sandy gonna put yourselves in danger like that! These Macho asshole will rape you.

Honey we're the bait!

No, I won't have it. I'm the cum-manding officer out here Mom. I'm not gonna let you guys sacrifice your vagina's. And I know you and Sandy are always look for a goodtime, but that's why you have Daddy at home so you can get laid whenever you want.

Mary, we won't have to get laid because we have Jane.

Ooooh great! Jane's your secret weapon? Ooh my Cock-God! Mom, how are you gonna deal with them, most of the Gruella Force are probably Non-Stud (NS) working dudes, not the brightest group?

Ooh Honey! We just have Jane strut amongst them giving off her *bitch-in-heat* Sissy **Pheromones** [4.D-G1.40] with her Sissy Poop, Jizzies and piss. And this will put an end to the human social grip on their penises. Humans are, sorry to say, pathetic when it cums to they're willpower against the ad-Dick-tive effect of the Sissy Vaganus®. Once they sense Jane's Sissy-Puss they'll forget all about our old human cunts they have back home.

Well Mom, Jane and I have done stuff like this on Church missions. So yeah, I think it's a good plan but dangerous! Who came up with it?

I did Honey! Mommy did! (Heather throws her chest out with pride).

Wow Mom! You're like a super spy chick now!

Hey! Like Mother like daughter! Mwah…

Mwah... Yep! I love you Mom. Ummm... Kissss... (Mom and Daughter French kiss. The Gurls always make-out with their Moms).

Yeah, it reminds me of a mission Jane and I did in British Columbia. And if you ever wonder how Canada was so easily Sissified. Well, we first bombed the shhh...it out of them with Bitch-Poop, but this is how it all started.

Juicy story I hope! Hmmm... Here babe! We have fresh **JizzyFizz**®. (Heather passes a bottle of flavor Man-Cream to Mary).

Thanks Mom. So, after bombing them, we rounded up some scanky local sluts then Jane drank and ate huge amounts of Stud-Cream. Next when the Hoes were surrounded by these big lumber-jack dudes, Jane just started dropping **Sissy-Poop**® turds and spraying Sissy-Piss and Jizzies all over the place! The affect was awesome!

Wow! Jane's a really trooper!

Oh yeah! Then they all whipped out their dicks and started humping me & Jane. We infected thousands of Canadian guys that week. They won't go near a Human pussy anymore! Unless of course they wanna knock-up their wife-bitch. Of course we had to send in the Latin American immigrant Army to round-up their Vaganus loving asses afterwards, but this is how Canada was Sissified!

[4.6] PREPARATION

Preparing for jungle combat...

Okay you ready **Jane**?

Mary I was born ready! Haa haaa…

JANE! I'm not kidding!

God-of-Cocks! Take it easy Mare, we've done this plenty of times, remember the lumber-jack Studs in Canada? We attract them with human sluts and then bait and switched. Once they dip they're pricks in us, we owned those dumb-ass humans!

Yeah, yeah… I know we've been on some outrageous missions. But Honey I need you to be careful. I mean I need you, I mean…

Hey! (Jane interrupts). I love you too! Stop worrying about me, okay?

Okay, I'll be in the cum-mand post, if something goes south on us I'm calling in the Sissy Army troops to extract you.

Geeeeez… Mare relax.

I'll relax when you're safe again.

Yes Mommy. MOM! Mary's bothering me again like she did when we were kids!

Kiss, kisss… I love you, don't you dare get hurt, Jane. (Mary hugs her tight). Mwah… Do you have the Pooop grenades?

Yes! Kiss…

Sissy First-Aid Kit, a **FAK** [25.5] and **Poop-Pellet**® [25.25.3] and **AVS**® Anti-Vagina Serum [4.D-G1.13a] and…

Yes! Yes! Yes! Okay let go! Haa... haa…Worry wart! Geeez…

You do look sexy in that Sergeants uniform, I love the camouflaged skirtini and the combat pumps. Fuck you turn me Jane, Ahhh… Oooh Baby. (Mary always gets super arouse when Jane wears soldier Gurl outfits) Mwah…

Kiss, kisss… Yeah I do look hot. These Contra dicks are gonna be more aroused than they've ever been in their lives. Ngh, Ahh, yeah I just needed to push out a poop turd Agh! So I can smear it all over my bottom. Ngh… Ahhh… (Jane poops in her hand and rubs it all over her scantily clad body). There! Now I'm ready, I got Sissy **Pheromones**® all over me! I wanna get this Latino Fuck-Out happening!

Whoa! Holy Cock-God Jane, calm down. Kiss Kisss…

You just had a Fuck-Out six days nine hours ago in Mecca.

Yeah, but I heard so many stories about Latino lovers. They say the Don Juan lovers can melt a Sissy Gurls heart. Huh! I'd like to see em try! I'll check it out for myself. You won't see me wimp out, I'm not afraid of these Casanova types. (Jane's all hyped up about the fight).

Ooooh! Save me! And I'm married to this nymph!

Shhh… shhh… (Radio sound) This is Point 6, we spotted the Contra-Vaganus soldiers. They're 9 klicks out. Shhh… shhh...

Shhh… shhh…. Okay Roger that! This is Jungle-Junk leader, enemy is approaching, so everybody get into your positions. Shhh… shhh….

[4.7] COMBAT

Somewhere in a Latin American jungle…

Hola Soldado! Necesitas algo que tengo? (Translation: Hello Soldier! You need something I have. Sandy has her skirt up with her bare naked pussy on displaying).

Oh si! Oh Bonita Puta! (Translation: Oh pretty whore. The Contra dudes just start humping Sandy from behind).

Aghhh! Aghhh! Oh yeah! Ti gusta mi cono? (Translation: you like my pussy). Jane! Oh yeah, it feels good! Yeah rub me there soldier, yeah! Uoooh! They're up my skirt Jane, start pissing and pooping all over the place Baby!

Okay Mom! Plop… plop... plop, pisssss….. (Jane let it all out).

Okay there they go! Smells great! They're following you Baby, go to the tented Whoring area and get into position. Holy Cock-Church there's dozens of these pheromone sniffing bastards! There's more than I expected. Shoot! Keep pooping Baby! Squirt some Jizzies on them!

Here Jane, I'll smear more of your poop all over you… Wow! They love sniffing and licking you! Awesome!

Yeah Mom! Here's another load Ngh! Plop... plop, pisssss…

Shhh… shhh… Jungle-Junk Leader do you read me, what's your status? Over. Shhh… shhh…

Shhh… shhh… There you go, follow the little Whore into the tent, awesome! Muy buena!

Shhh… shhh… Yes, this is Jungle-Junk Mommy-One, it's all working, and they're jerking-off while following Sergeant Jane into the *Tent-of-Love* [25.19] over! Shhh… shhh… Ten-Four… Shhh… shhh…

Shhh… shhh… this is Jungle-Junk Mommy-Two I need assistance, there's too many of them! I got Contras humping me! Shhh… shhh…

Shhh… shhh… This is Mommy-One I'm in route to you Mommy-Two! Shhh… shhh… Get some poop grenades over here ASAP!

Shhh… shhh… Agh! They… Ahhhh… PENETRATED Ahhh… me! I've been penetrated! Agh! Pisssss… (Sandy sprays the Contra soldiers in the face with Sissy **Pheromones** [4.D-G1.40] to get them off of her). Pisssss… Ahhh! Shit! Get your grubby little Non-Stud dick out of my cunt!

Shhh… shhh… MEDIC! I'm in need of a Medic over here NOW! Over! Shhh… shhh…

Shhh… shhh… Mommy-Two requesting emergency field douche-out equipment over! My Chastity-Belt popped up and I got enemy Jizzzied in my Baby-Maker! Over! Shhh… shhh…

Shhh… shhh… Where's my support! Dam it! I broke a heel!

Shhh… shhh… This is Jungle-Junk Leader, evacuate to the Tent-of-Love area now! Over! Shhh… shhh…

Shhh…shhh…This is Mommy-One. Mommy-Two took a load! We need to medevac her the-hell-out of here NOW!

Shhh… shhh… I called in for an air strike! We're gonna carpet bomb this area with Sissy pheromones. Over!

Shhh… shhh… There won't be a vagina-lover left when we're done with them!

Shhh… shhh… Fuck! There's thousands of them! Their like ants! Ahhh… Got Jizzies in my eye! Get us out of here!

Shhh… shhh… This is Jungle-Junk Leader I repeat, retreat to the Tent-of-Love! We'll air-left you and your unit out of there.

Shhh… shhh… Dam it! Where the hell is the Spermicide!

Shhh… shhh… Fall-back that's an order!

[4.8] TENT-OF-LOVE

Hours of Cock-to-Cunt combat later…

Jane! Jane! (**Heather** pats Jane on the face to try and revive her) It's Heather! Shhhh…it! She's out-cold! Those bastards fucked her out! MEDIC! Pisssss… (Heather sprays **Vaginaicide** on the enemy soldier). Dam it! That was my last pheromones spray can and my guns out of poop pellets! Fuck! We're screwed or will be! Oh **Sandy**! This place is all Jizzed-out.

Yeah Heather just put me down. (Sandy says in a faint voice). I'm covered in it Baby! I took too many penetrations. Leave me behind, Heather you go with Jane!

Huh! No way Girlfriend!

Heather, I'll attract them away from the **Helivac** with my tits and ass! I've done it before and do it again!

Haa… Girlfriend Kiss... Not gonna happen! I'm not leaving without you!

Chuf, chuf, chuf…. (Helicopter sound).

You hear that? They're cuming Baby! The medevac is here! Me and you Baby! Whoa! You fucker! I'll show you how a Girl can fight! Aaaagh! Ahhh... There you son of bitch! (Heather kicked the enemy soldier in the balls to defend their position).

Sister **Heather**, I'm **Master Sergeant Dueme** the medevac is here and we gotta go now Ma'am! There's gonna be an air strike in a few minute. This whole village is gonna be covered in poop!

Okay, I'm not leaving without these two! We can get those two out on the next air-left Ma'am! There's only room for three of us. We gotta go now!

I'll stay behind! Sniff... Sniff... You take these two to safety now soldier!

Nah, Sister! I'll stay, you leave with them!

Bless you Gurl!

Just doing my duty Mam! Go now!

Dueme what's your outfit soldier?

Army Sissy Corps 6th Battalion 9th Infantry Brigade 69th Special Sissy Forces Regiment, Fort Didher.

Chuf, chuf, chuf... Go! Go! Go!

I'll stay behind and take them up my cooch till you're free from here!

Chuf, chuf, chuf... (The helicopter takes off leaving Dueme surrounded by Contra fighters humping her).

Two days later, back at base…

Okay let's wrap it up I gotta head back.

Yes Captain.

Oh and make sure the locals get enough hole.

Captain Dune we're running short of registered holes at the temporary Whoring Stations we setup in the Jungles.

Well, what about sex machines? Yeah we got them and we rounded up all the fagots in the area, but the locals are infected so they prefer real Sissy Vaganus to either vagina or ass-pussy.

Ahhh… I was hoping it wouldn't cum to this. Use the ASB if you have to but only sixty-nine LCTs per day each. We don't wanna wear those precious little holes out before they're official Whoring age. Just make sure you douche they're holes out afterwards.

Yes Mam! Anything else Captain?

Yeah, just one more long thing Soldier.

Whoa! Aghh! Wow! (Mary opens her uniforms blouse and undoes her front bra clip exposing her huge tits) I wasn't expecting that Mam! (The young Stud Soldier is standing there with his mouth open staring at Mary's stunning body).

It's okay Lieutenant, what's the matter? You've never seen a Sissy Captain bend over for you before?

No Ma'am! Ahhh…. (He anxiously tries to get his pants off).

Okay! Well let's get to it solider; I have a plane on the tarmac waiting for me. Agh! Yeah! Good Boy! Agh! Yeah! There you go! Oooooh! I need your nice big man sausage! Agh!

On the runway…

Sandy, Mom it's all yours. This Cunt-trie and possibly many others in Latin America will be saved from the old religious morality soon. Viva Vaganus!

Well Mary, we got a lot of work to do setting up other insurgent teams. But, we'll penetrate deeper and deeper into their moral fabric and then it's just a matter of time before it be cums an American Sissy ad-Dick-ted world. We'll own Latin America.

Yep! Our first **ASB**® shipment is due to arrive tomorrow. So you'll be distributing them to the villagers who became infected in the battle.

Right, right! And we're holding our first Holy Cockolic Church (HCC) services this Sunday. So yeah, it's happening real fast. We're signing the locals up to do Sissy breeding training.

Excellent Mom!

And of course we don't call it that. The locals think the ASB are orphaned humans. I mean the Latinos don't know the human looking babies we're giving them are actually Sissies. I mean if they notice the tail bone stub protruding from the top of their ass we'll just call it an abnormality.

Right Mom! And hey forget the side effects of Sissy offspring raping all the male members of their families and then going on to drain the balls of the rest of the village or town. Minor problem!

Exactly they call it a, grass-roots movement.

Yeah, one dick, one Sissy, one acquired asset at a time. Well, gotta go! See you two soon. Mwah...

Okay they got Jane's stretcher loaded into the jet! Mwah...

Mwah... Yep! I gotta go! I love you Mom! I love you both!

I love you too Mary. Mwah... Please take care of Jane for me.

Sandy! Your daughter is the love of my life, I would never think of not taking care of her! Mwah...

You two stay close to each other down here in Latin America. And no more combat missions, that's an order. And if a guy cums up to you and says his name is Casanova. RUN!

Captain Dune we have to takeoff. Gotta go you two! Mwah...

Mwah... Okay but let's pray!

Aaaah! Geeeeez... Sandy with the praying.

May the Holy Cock save you and Jane and be guided inside of you through times of hardon-ship Amen...

Sandy Mom. Mwah... We'll see you back State-side soon. Stay out of trouble please! Kiss Kisss... Bye Honey! Mwah...

Chapter 5: Back in DC

[5.1] COMMITTEE

Several Months later at the LCT Meeting...

Ms. **Dune**! Let me read this report which crossed my desk this morning from our operatives in Latin America (LA). I quote:

The Russians have globally cornered the American Sissy Baby black-market trade.

End quote. I don't know what else can be more disturbing then hearing this. In other words, our American assets are going to the Russians for free. We're literally giving **ASB**® [4.D-G3.12] to them!

Chairperson **Goldberg** I know the figures sound bad. (Seymour, Jane's cousin, has always had feelings for Mary).

Bad! Seriously Director **Dune**! These numbers are eating a hole in our pocket. Money goes out, but nothing cums in! Why do we give, and I repeat, give away Sissy babies to the Latin Americans. I mean seriously it's like pouring money down the drain!

Chairperson I beg to differ. I have evidence it is working from our troops stationed down there and the Holy Cockolic Church (HCC) Missionaries, who prove distribution of the ASB®.

Oooh! And how so Director **Dune**, what's the penetration?

It correlates with the increase in membership at the HCC parishes in many of the LA Cunt-tries. The increased parish sizes have also increased the amount of penetration detection equipment, the **PDE**® [4.D-G1.14] installed in those Cunt-tries. And the more penetration equipment we have installed the greater the profit potential for the USA Inc.

Right, right... Because the **PDE**® is linked to the American banking system and we collect a fee when a Sissy hole is penetrated.

Yes referring to the **Sissydom**® Manual, they have permission to penetrate the Sissy (**HO**) if and only if the male has performed work.

Correct! Providing they have the minimum amount of MO required.

Yes Sir. Typically the locals down there earn their MO by working either for the USA Inc. or our subsidiaries, because we took over all the State run enterprises down there. So the USA Inc. benefits from the earned-income labor and the worker benefits from the **Vaganus**®.

Exactly! And we double dip into their pockets by selling them basic essential to live on. Then it's a rinse-n-repeat. Referring to [12.L1.2] Section 12, Appendix I, List 1, the HOMO formula works, where HO is the Whore,

$$HO + MO = increased\ productivity$$

Dune, I like you. (Seymour winks at Mary).

Thank you Sir.

Dune, you know I'm related to your wife **Jane Goldberg**?

Yes Sir! I'm fully aware of this. My wife and you are kissing cousins.

Right, right... I mean not to say it had anything to do with your political appointment, it was completely coincidental that you were approved as the Director of the **POOP** [4.D-G8.1] program.

Yes Sir. And I admire you for the work you've done at the DHMC to implement the **MSES**®. [4.D-G2.1]

Well thank you! So, now that we've finished patting each other on the back. Let's move on! So Director, than you're saying, we're completely reliant on the HCC to increase penetration and installation of the Penetration Detection Equipment, the **PDE** [4.D-G1.14]?

Yes Chairmen! This is pretty much how it works down there. And this is geopolitically and sexually. The Latinos are religious and our control is all about them switching their affiliation to Sissydom® related church orgasmizations like the HCC. But the war against the Latino vagina is fierce. The combat is village to village and bed to bed. But the Contra-Vaganus fighters are getting clever. They know they have no defense against the, all ad-Dick-tive, chemical substance of the American Sissy Bitches Pheromones®. I mean the **COPS**, the Cream or Poop Severity is explicit [18.13a].

Ms. Dune you're speaking about, **WMP** weapons of massive Poopalation [25.7] were the excreted Sissy chemical triggers a social response? This is also known as horniness.

Yes Chairmen. But **DOM**® [1.A2.1] Sissies like me have little or no effect on the human males. So the Contras started wearing gas masks to break through behind the lines and disrupt the Sissy supply chains, commandeering supplies of Chastity-Belts®, bottled sperm for feeding the Sissy babies, etc.

I see, I see.... Huh! Well what can we do about it Dune?

Ahh… We've started several programs. We're shipping tons of Sissy-Poop® to Latin America in an effort to spread the Sissy **pheromones**. It's similar to what we did many years ago to with the US dollar. Just pump billions and billions of dollars down there to developing nations to hook them into dollar dependence.

Okay Dune, so is this a problem? After the Second World War, (WW2) the USA Inc. had the world by the balls and then we squeezed them hard creating a Debt-Peonage.

Huh! Yeah, even though this atrocity is not mentioned in our school textbook.

Director Dune! Yeah, Americans are vultures, so what! Okay, so back to the problem, just hit them with more Sissy **pheromones**!

Yes! I hear you. But this is a production problem. Because unlike the US dollar where we just pressed a button and created money out of thin-fucking-air! Bitch-Poop though is only produced out of the Sissies Vaganus®, emphasis on anus. Like I said, only the Bitch-Poop® is infectious the DOM pheromones are inert to humans. Oddly enough the DOM-Poop® sexually turns on FEM-Cock® ladies, but this is an entirely different issue.

Okay Dune! So what the heck are you doing about the shortage?

Well, to increase the Bitch-Poop® volume for shipping, we've installed poop collection bins next to the other recycling containers. We're also in the process of aerial pheromone spraying, inoculating the water and food supplies. We're also working on several invasive methods like the brute-force tactical jungle strikes we've been doing.

Yes, yes, I read about the mission you cummanded several months ago. I salute you Director Dune and all the other military service personal in the United States Army Sissy Reserve for their valiant efforts which make America safe from non-Sissy Cunt-tries.

Thank you Sir.

Well Dune, I need to empty my nut-sack. Let's take a short break and continue the meeting in about 69 minutes from now.

[5.2] BLACK MARKET

LCT Meeting continued…

Okay! So getting back to the issues we have with the Russians.

Yes, well we know 69 percent of the **ASB**® supplied down there end up being traded for Russian Vodka and jobs. Jobs on Mars are the highest paying in the world, so naturally the Central and South Americans are deciding to swap out their sexually active American Sissy baby for real earnings.

Okay, but where do the Russians dump the merchandise?

Oh! Well this is interesting, the Arab world is the largest buyer of illegal ASB® in the world.

Haaa haa ha… Yes this is ironic considering the Islamic world declared a Holy Jihad on all of Sissydom®.

Right, well yeah, but this was only after the incident several months ago caused by the infiltration of an Anti-Vagina infected Sissy. The infected Sissy caused an outbreak of **Vaginaosis**®. [4.D-G1.13a]

Wait, what is it?

Oooh **Vaginaosis**? It's a new bacterium which was created recently by American bio-scientists at the Deep Advanced Raw Penetration Agency, **DARPA** [25.26.1]. It's not fatal and is no more harmful than the common cold. But it can be discomforting for a short time. Rashes form on a male penis after having sex with a human female. But the males are not affected if they have **Sissy-Sex** [15-69.7].

Huh! That's amazing!

Well yes! The good folks at DARPA have cum up with all kinds of ways to cripple those who do not agree with us. It's survival of the fittest.

Vaginaosis would account for there being a buying spree of Sissy Gurls® by Muslims after the Islamic Hajj this past year. But Chairman I really don't think the Russians are the problem.

Wow! And what makes you think this, Dune?

Well I believe they're obviously trying to disrupt the American efforts to unite the world through Sissydom®. But we're only trying to bring peace to the world through the increase in sexual pleasure. And as usual American profit is just a byproduct of our efforts.

Right! So what's wrong with that?

I agree Chairperson Goldberg. What I was getting at is the Russians are doing us a favor.

Huh? How so? You just stated they're disrupting our cash flow!

Well the ASB® is only being relocated by the Russians.

Huh? I'm sorry I'm still confused with your logic Director Dune.

It's like this. The ASB® is sent to the buyer, and the Baby will spread pheromones to anyone anywhere! And it doesn't care or even know who she affected. Okay so it's an Arab instead of a Latin American, should we care? No, the proliferation of Vaganus® sex orientation of the entire planet will happen. The Russians are just spreading the American Sissy seed for us. Clap, clap, clap… (The whole Cum-mittee applauds).

Thank you, Cum-mittee members. So the real issue here is, are we concerned with the distribution of the American Vaganus® or are we shooting for the installation of the American payment system?

Like we were saying, years ago during the fascist controlled USA there was the SWIFT system. Now the only payment system to survive is the sixty-ninth generation UnionPay and the Cross-Border Interbank Payment System (CIPS). So this whole thing about the Vaganus® and sexual orientation is really about control of the money hegemony.

I mean American Vaganus® is like the new Atomic bomb.

Haaaa haaa, haa… Ms. Dune you're funny.

No I'm actually quite serious! Back in the day, the USA was the only Cunt-tree with an atomic bomb and we were feeling mighty tough. And then came the H-bomb and we were feeling like we could control the world. But then other Cunt-tries developed the H-bomb too. So really it made no difference.

Director Dune are you going somewhere with this?

Yes, yes, please bear with me! Okay. You see, eventually there may be other Cunt-tries in the world creating and breeding Sissies.

Ooooh, Oooh, Ooh... (The Cum-mittee is in shock at the thought of a non-American Sissy). Impossible! Haa ha... Never happen!

Sure, sure... I know, hard for me to fathom a Bitch from somewhere else being anything like my sweet Sissy wife Jane. But it might happen!

In the decades to cum Sissydom® is likely to spread throughout Central and South America. And then beyond to places like Southeast Asia, Africa, Russia, India, Europe who knows maybe even all of Eurasia and possibly the Middle-East. Again, as the US dollar had, back in the fascist era, after the war and the withdrawal from the Bretton Woods agreement. Right, not to mention the Petro-Dollar.

Right! Who is to say if they won't invent a better Sissy a Sexier more profitable version. For example the Chinese Yuan eventually overcame the US dollar as the dominant currency. And yeah it's hard to believe, but true. When and if they invent a Sissy, perish the thought, will this Cunt-tree, will the United States Inc. have a payment system installed in the majority of people in the ever expanding sexual Shangri-La we call Sissydom.

Clap, clap, clap… (The Cum-mittee applauds).

Okay! What you're saying Director is, now we're benefiting by being the only one on the block, the only Cunt-tree producing the Vaganus®. And mind you, American Sissy-Puss will probably always be the best quality hole money can buy. But this could change and when it does the USA Inc. has to have the payment system installed on the most participants.

Yes Chairmen. We have the, Sissy Sexual Activity Auto-Accounting System, the **SSAAAS** [4.D-G1.26]. It's been tested and ready to go global. Hell it even has language settings for our non-English speaking Sissydom participants.

Muy bueno!

Si Senior! And the signal transmitting antennas of the SSAAAS are embedded inside each Sissy hole. And also around all the penises of workmen, which keeps an accurate account of who and how many times a Sissies hole has been penetrated for the good of all of us.

Right Dune! Dependence is what it's all about.

Exactly Chairperson, the SSAAAS is a great system. But in the future are we going to be in control of the payment system or are we going to be cum a has-been Nation, an **Empty Nation** filled with FEMA camps and horny unemployed middle-class humans?

Hmmm… Ahhh… Is she Pro-Stud or not Seymour? (The Cum-mittee is debating Mary's loyalty). Huh! Sissies, huh! Who is she for? (More grumbling from the Oligarchical bureaucrats).

From the grumbling I'm hearing, I take it none of you have been to a FEMA camp or a Breeding farm?

No Director Dune! Nor should we need to! (Senator McCuntell exclaims). I don't believe any of us have ever visited a camp or zone. But we're Law-makers, there's really no need for folks of our statue to be concerned with workers no less unemployed ones.

Wow! (Now Mary has to deal with bigots). Okay let me explain my scheme to the Cum-mittee. When I think of the SSAAAS I see three parts, (a) Sissy transmission antennas, and (b) workmen transmission antennas and (c) the receiver side equipment of the controlling parties. The problem lies in the part (b).

Why is that Director?

Well as we've experienced, it's pretty easy to get distribution of POOP babies to nations. Either on the premise of it being a humanitarian cause to adopt poor American babies, or in an impoverished Cuntree ASB is given as humanitarian aid in corporation with the Cockolic Church, where the parents make 6.9 percent on the transactions.

Yes and so this is all working out fine right?

Yeah! Despite the Russians.

We're increasing our livestock breeding and distribution channels with pre-installed antennas. No problem. But we also need the antenna RFID chip implanted on the worker-class human participants. The Sissy side is no problem all ASB produced on the Breeding-Farm ship with pre-load, enabled equipment. The human side is where the problem is. For (b) we have to work within the borders of the Non-Sissydom Cunt-tree.

This means, setting up clandestine operations. These stem from, underground Vaganus® Addiction outreach groups, to pseudo HCC Anti-Vagina teams. The groups are equipped with the antenna supplies and embedding specialists to install the devices on the Vaganus® hungry participants.

Alright, let me just get this straight you want the USA Inc. government to sponsor black operation missions to non-Sissy Cunt-tries?

Yes! We need more Black Ops!

Okay Director Dune, I think we're done here for today but I need you to make an appointment to see me about this matter behind closed doors. Okay thank you everyone, this meeting of the LCT Implementation Cummittee is concluded.

Wow, I don't think it went over so well, Jane.

Ahhhh... Mare you can't win them all! Kiss. I love you.

Ooh Jane, sometimes I feel like I'm the only one taking it up-the-cooch. These Cunt-gressmen are just a bunch of wealth bigots, hypocrites and con-artist.

Cheer up! Let's go home and I'll comfort your big DOM worries away. Mwah... (Jane, only being four feet tall, hugs Mary around her waist).

Yeah cum on! I need to get out of these six inch pumps and get a good fisting from my precious little Bitch... Ummm... Kiss... kisss. I love you too Jane. Mwah...

[5.3] BOOTY CAMP

Days later at the FUCIT campus Sissy-ROTC...

Okay listen up you little queer lady boys! I'll show you the most common combat field technique. Just imagine these dildos are the enemy pricks. The drill goes like this. Repeat after me!

Kiss, Grab, Insert...!!!...

Kiss, Grab, Insert...!!!...

Kiss, Grab, Insert...!!!...

First kiss them on their prick-head like so, Kissss! (Drill-Sergeant Cunty demonstrates to the Sissy Gurl recruits the basics with a rubber dildo).

Second, grab the penis hard, and insert it up your juicy little fuckhole! Like so! Ahhh... (Cunty mounts, the extremely large, rubber dildo in one plunge of her twat). Yeah! Now, I wanna see how you elegant little pansies do it! Okay begin!

Kiss, Grab, Insert...!!!...

You got that Private! (Sarah struggles to get the colossal size dildo up her cooch). I don't see any enthusiasm HERE! What are you a dainty little LADY? Or are you a lean, mean, man fucking machine! Sissy **BITCH**! What are you? (Cunty is shouting directly into Sarah's eye).

I'm a bitch. (Sarah shaking with fear of the Amazon size Drill Sergeant screaming cum-mands in her ear, replies in an almost inaudible voice).

I CAN'T HEAR YOU!

I'm a bitch. (Slightly louder).

YES! YOU'RE A BITCH! YOU WERE BORN A BITCH AND YOU WILL ALWAYS BE A BITCH…!!!...

OW! (Cunty presses Sarah's shoulders and impales her onto the immense phallic object).

Pissssss… Agh! Yeah that's right bath in my piss Bitch! Ahhh… Ahhh… Pisssss…(Cunty empties her bladder onto Sarah).

Hit the showers all of you! I don't wanna look at your miserable little queer Sissy asses anymore!

Yes Ma'am! (All the Gurls shout as they scamper off to the shower room).

After the drill…

Wow Jane! (Mary & Jane are both in disbelief of the cruelty shown by the Drill sergeant). How did it cum to this?

Not sure partner. It wasn't like this when we were kids or when we were in the Sissy-ROTC. Geeez… What went wrong?

Got no idea, but I'm gonna find out what! (Mary is fuming).

Maybe it's because after the Beijing Climax Accord, the BCA [4.D-G4.18] the military started getting Sissies involved in soldiering. They finally started training Sissies to fight Sex-Wars. The world replace lethal force with sex.

Huh! We both know it's a fantasy because Sissies aren't violent. So the fight just be cums the fuck.

Mary did you noticed all the recruits were Bitches, no DOM Gurls in the ranks?

Yes Jane, you know I notice inequality amongst Sissies. I'm on the Sissy equal rights cum-mittee.

And the Sergeant was a little over the top with the shouting. The Gurls were all crying and shivering. Pssss... I saw some of them wetting their panties!

Jizz-Us! For the Love-of-Cock! Just what I thought! Look at this pathetic sight. Here's the Officers lounge area where all the DOMs are just sitting around sipping on their fancy flavored cummy lattes. Huh! This makes me sick! Spineless DOM Gurls who won't defend their enlisted Bitches!

Major Dune! (The Officer Sissy-Salutes). Mwah... Mwah...

Mwah... Mwah... (Mary salutes back).

I'm Second Lieutenant Ann **Dickmee** (EN10) the superior officer here at the FUCIT Sissy ROTC [25.17.1] training center, good to meet you Ma'am. I've heard so much about you Ma'am, the Latin American Jungle-Junk mission, you're the Director of POOP. It's an honor to have you visiting us.

Yeah, yeah, Dickmee thanks for your praise. Look we're here to give lectures in Sissy tactical field operations, but what we just saw out in the yard is revolting! It's a disgrace to the Sissy Corps! [25.1] Slap! (Mary slaps Dickmee in the face lightly).

Ma'am! I just follow orders from my Superiors. I'm not the one who came up with all this drill training crap! I think our Sissies are more than capable of handling themselves in most situations without the training.

Well, can they handle humiliation?

They've all had, FO, POM and Gangbang (GB)? How about Sissy Code of Whoring Ethics, the **SCWE** [15] training.

Yes Ma'am Major Dune! Fuck-Out (FO), Piss-on-Me (POM) and GB all standard training for Sex-War combat.

And this sexual deprived human female Instructor? What's her name?

Drill-Sergeant Cunty.

Yeah Cunty, her screaming in the recruits face stuff is all leftover from the old human side of the US Military [25]. These Gurls have all been through the National Sissy Training Program, the **NSTP** [4.D-G2.7].

Yes Ma'am. Sniffff….

Are you crying Dickmee? (Mary firmly says up close in Dickmee's face).

Snifff… No Ma'am! Sorry to disappoint you ma'am! (Dickmee snaps to attention and whips her face while trying to hold back a tear). Snifff…

Right. Well I'm gonna talk with the Military folks back in Washingcum about this and they're not gonna like what I have to say about it. And Dickmee. Mwah… (Mary give an apologetic kiss on the Officers cheek). Sorry I was rough with you. You're a good soldier. We need Gurls like you.

[5.5] PIMPS

The Gurls revisit their Mistresses (Pimps)...

Gurls! What did I tell you about this? You just have to accept it. The more we incorporate the US military into the fight against the vagina in far off Cunt-tries of the world, the more we have to play their game at home. Sure I don't like the human female drill sergeants degrading the poor Sissy recruits. Although, I think the Bitches actually enjoy a little abuse. But hey! It's all part of the game!

But Cardinal....

Ahhhh... No buts Jane. These military brutes are not to be messed with. They're violent and also horny. So play the sex card Jane. These seasoned soldiers at the booty camps are human females and have an axe to grind with Sissies. But the Stud officers back in Washingcum running the military machine are like every other male creature in nature they have a weakness for the pussy hole.

Ah huh! Brilliants! (Jane exclaims).

Yes! So, if you really want to control the situation, when you Gurls are negotiating with the military guys, rub your Vaganus® in front of them. It will give off Sissy Pheromones. And you know what happens after that.

Yeah! You're right Cardinal, animals are vulnerable. Hell! Cats and dogs chase me down the street trying to hump me. Humans are not any different, they're animals too!

Exactly sweetheart. And you've been playing with me for an hour, so Gurls now take your Holy Cum-Union Aghhh...!!!... Yes... I love you Gurls so much! Ahhh.... And miss you dearly. Kisss...

After servicing their Mistresses...

Lordess Rimme. May I ask a question?

Yes my dear Mary.

I need advice about something.

Oooh! Is Cardinal **Jackeroff** feeding you enough FEM sperm?

No, no... We're fine in that department, she feeds us well.

Than speak your mind Child you may confess anything to me.

Ahhh... We really need to get the electronic gear, the PDE installed on the human participants in these non-Sissified Cunt-tries. Otherwise this whole POOP thing is going to blow-up in my face. We have the one side of the equation working by distributing the Sissies babies from the farm. But the human participant side is just slowly developing, too slow actually. Unless we equip the humans with the technology to transmit the signal to the Vaganus® during and after coitus, we're domed!

Oooh Mary! My dear sweet Mary, there is a solution. Mwah...

Oh! My Lordess! Please if you can help me please do so!

This is what will happen, Mary. We have infiltrated the hospital and medical professions throughout the world with CI & HCC members. The Church has a special program to train doctors and nurses in the art of installing the transmitting devices into the human patience's. It's called, Doctors without Booty, **DWB** [23.39].

Wow! Awesome! But how, how do they do it behind enemy lines?

Oh! Well it's quite simple Mary. For example, let's say some doofus goes to the doctor for a common illness, a phallic object crammed up their ass or something. So while it's being remove, unbeknownst to the patient, Presto-Change-O! They secretly had an antenna and micro-chip implanted around their dick or vagina.

Wow! Is that possible? I love you Rimme. What would I do without you? Kiss… Mwah…

Yes, yes… This happens all the time, Mary. Kiss your Lordess. Kiss my erection like a good Gurl. Kiss, kiss… Yes, this is the appropriate gratitude. Worship what you desire most. Ahhhh… Kiss… Agh! Good Gurl! Mwah….

Now Mary, this is all between us.

What do you mean, your Holiness?

Agh! Okay when you get back the District of Cuntcumbia, to DC and meet with **Seymour**, this was all your idea. The HCC cooperation, the Doctors-without-Booty and Nurses doing the implants. You got that?

Yep! Kisss... Kisss… (The Gurls kiss their Mistresses goodbye).

Have a good trip back to DC Gurls. Kiss…

[5.6] DHMC OFFICE

Ahhhh… Cum in Director **Dune**.

Oooh! Please Assistant Director **Goldberg**, call me Mary.

Fine! Mwah… And please call me **Seymour**. And thanks for taking the time to cum by.

Ahh… Yeah… But Seymour to be honest with you, I've been nervous about meeting with you on this matter.

Oh! Mary please! We're colleagues there's no need to get all worried about this stuff. Everything works out in the end. And my dear, your rear end is looking might fine. Mwah… (Seymour goes in for a squeeze and some tongue action). Ummm…

Mwah… Haaa haa… Oooh Seymour, you're a very sweet man. (Mary passes her hand over the face of Seymour). Mwah… Let's talk! This is what I wanted to assure you about today.

Mary! I got your back on this. And how's Jane? Mwah…

Haa haaa... She's fine! You know Jane. I think she's doing most of your staff in the cumference room as we speak.

Haaa... Yeah, Goldberg kids are a wild bunch. All the Goldberg Girls or Gurls are on the wild side.

Well Sandy, Jane's Mom is the most caring, compassionate human women I ever meet. And yeah, like you said, quite on the wild side.

Haa... haaa... Oh yeah! Quite wild is an understatement. But hey what can I do for you today besides giving a massage to your cooch?

Ahhh… It feels sooo good Seymour. Mwah… Seymour I told you and the Cum-mittee about the problem we're having with the human factor in the distribution chain.

Yeah Mary! And quite frankly I have no idea how you're going to solve the problem, other than needing approval to cross borders illegally and still be funded. This is a tough one. I mean, the USA Inc. government is hated in most cunt-tries. I hope you have a plan!

Yes, I have one Seymour.

Wow! Well please tell me more. And here Mary sit on my lap. Uncle Seymour needs to park his manhood in your nice warm tunnel-of-love. Cum on! Don't be shy. (Seymour cups Mary's ass in his hand).

Yeah, well I have a plan to go behind the enemy lines and implant the equipment needed to make this work.

Yeah... Ummm... Kisss... Tell Uncle Seymour everything.

Ohhh! Seymour Ummm… It feels good. Yeah feel me up Dude! Unhook my bra. Yeah feel-up my tits. (Seymour is slobbering away on Mary's huge nipples).

Ahh… Yes Mary, we're related now. Mwah… Your wife is my cousin. And you know what this means?

Ahhh… let me guess. You're going to implant your now fully erect related man muscle into my quivering lovehole?

Exactly! Aghhh…. Yeah… Kisss, Kiss. Mwah… Mwah…

Several orgasms later…

Wow! The stories about you Seymour are true. Kiss… Kisss.

Of course my dear. And Mary, I'm more to you now than a cousin, lover and Chairman.

Huh?

Mary, I know people. (Seymour says with an all knowing grin on his face).

Pardon me? Like who?

I know **Rimme**, **Yaoi** hell I even know the Cock-Pope!

Ahhh… Professors Yaoi and Rimme. They were the academic advisor for Jane and I. How you know the Pope is a mystery though. And how in the world does everyone get to know the Pope except for me and Jane?

Haaa, haa, ha… Relax, I'll get an appointment for you Gurls with her, the Pope and I are tight! And when I said I know Rimme and Yaoi, I meant, know of them, hint, hint. The catacombs under the Sissyology Building. The secret harems, what they have strapped to their tights and…

Okay! That's enough information! Huh! You know they're FEMs?

Yep! And they're both Pimps. Mary, like I said, I know a lot of stuff about a lot of people!

Okay, so I take it you know we're Nuns in the HCC?

Oh yeah Mary, let me stop you there, I know everything! I mean everything! Most of which I learned from research I did for my book. **RFAP**© [21.B.1].

The Rise and Fall of the American Penis

Yeah! I read your book, several times. It was mandatory reading back in college. **Jizz-Us**® [9.I3.0] you know everything?

Yep! I know you're scheduled to knock-up my cousin Sandy to create a new Super Hybrid Sissies the **Pussucock** [4.D-G3.24.1] Shhh…it! That would make you my sister-in-law, I think? Hey I even know the hour the conception is going to happen!

Okay Seymour, so, let's just figure you know everything. Do you know my plan how we're going to infiltrate into non-Sissydom Cunt-tries?

Well No! Not actually.

I see. Okay well regardless, this is my plan. We're going to strategically place medical doctors and nurses into or from these Cunt-tries, and they're gonna be our boots on the ground. They'll install the **PDE** [4.D-G1.14] and **SSAAAS** [4.D-G1.26] equipment on the unknowing participants.

Awesome! It's a fantastic plan. The thing about the grass-roots movements to allure want-a-be **Vaganus**® lovers is rubbish! It wasn't going to work, there's not enough traction. Don't get me wrong, there's some merit to the Vaganus® ad-Dick-tion recovery program scheme. Allure them into a program to kick the **Sissy-Sex**® habit. It works, Alcoholic Anonymous AA, drug abuse rehab, they're all effective. But we're trying to reach out to the entire population of these Cunt-tries not the small ad-Dick-ted sector of it. Besides, the folks you attract in the, how to kick the Vaganus® habit is the bottom portion.

Right, the freaks, perverts, recovering gays and lesbians, pedophiles, erotica and political novelists, closet crossdressers, usury bankers, wanna-be-fags, game-show hosts like Donald (the douche-bag) president, civil servants, human sissies, college students, politicians, **FEMA** [4.D-G7.13] camp refugees, urban planners, the dregs of society.

Huh! So Seymour, I assume you're with me on this?

Absolutely Mary! We'll give you everything you need, just ask. I mean everything you need sweetheart. Mwah...

Ooooh Seymour! Kisss... Yeah for that I have a Pimp. But hey! For a guy with a relatively small dick, you're one of the best lovers I've ever had! Mwah... You'll be seeing me soon and often. Kissss... Mwah...

On the way out of office...

Hey Honey! Mwah... Did you enjoy yourself with the boys in the office?

Oh yeah! The office staff shafts are awesome and the manager is a super sexy Chinese-American. I invited her over to play with us later.

Cool! Kiss... Is Jacky downstairs waiting for us with the car?

Yep! I got your back... Kissss...

[5.7] HUMANS

Outside of the DHMC Building…

We Need Sex! We Need Sex! We Need Sex! Girls! What do we got?

Pussy Power...!!!...

What the hell is this?

Holy-Poop! Its human females protesting about not getting enough sex.

No More Sissies! No More Sissies! No More Sissies! (The VAC women are shouting their protest slogan).

Yeah well I feel they should protest. (Jane has a supportive attitude about disadvantaged folks, having been one for most of her life).

Whoa! Jane duck! (Mary saves Jane from getting hit in the head by flying dildos) Geeez… It almost hit you! Dang-it! They're throwing dildos at us!

No More Vaganus, No More Vaganus... (The hatred for the vagina substitutes is heard in the chanting).

I would be mad too if I wasn't getting enough at home. (Jane shouts back at the women in support of their cause waving her fists in the air). I'd be in the streets protesting.

Jane you never have enough sex. And besides, they're humans! They don't need it as often as we do. Quick get in Jane! Jacky just get us out of here!

Sure thing Boss!

Sissies! Look Sissies getting into that car! Fuck you Sissies! Crash! (The females are throwing hard rubber dildos at the Gurls chaffered luxury sedan). Crash! (They're damaging the car, smashing the glass). Crash! Crash! Crash! (Sound of breaking glass) Whoa!

Stop fucking monkeys! Stop fucking monkeys... (The chanting continues).

Pussy Power! (As the car pulls away Jane leans out of the car window and shouts out in support of their struggle) Pussy Power! Crash! Jane get in! Crash! Crash! (Breaking glass).

Vagina Rules! Vagina Rules! Vagina Rules!...

Wow! Crash! (Smashing glass as Jacky their driver speeds away). Holy-Cock! Crash! Wow! Right in front of a Federal Building! This is Washingcum DC, I feel like we're back in the Jungle again. Crash! Crash!

We're only Sissy Gurls. Jacky what's going on?

Oh this is happening all over the Cunt-tree. There's a big Nation-wide protest against Sissies.

But we didn't hurt anybody.

It's not the way they see it Mary. These females haven't been getting sex from their husbands because they're ad-Dick-ted to

Vaganus®. They just don't want the vagina anymore, unless they're trying to get the wife pregnant. But they're protesting a lot of things. Government issued Chastity-Belts, Sissy Dress Code, Sissy Rights, all kinds of stuff. It's not so safe to be a Sissy anymore. Especially in **Baltimore**, they're burning effigies of Sissies there!

Cocky! Cocky! Cocky! Wooo! (Jane's cell phone ringtone is a popular song in 2254) Hello. Yeah this is **Jane**. Oh Shhhh…it! Okay I'm on the way! **Jacky** get us to the Johns Hopkinky hospital. My Mom was brought into the emergency room!

Jane? What's going on? Talk to me! (Mary hugs Jane).

They flew her and your Mom in from Rio de Janeiro. Your Mom is alright, Sniff, Sniff… Shhhh…it! Fucking salvation missions for the Church!

Hang on Honey. (Mary holds Jane tight)

[5.8] EMERGENCY

At Johns Hopkinky hospital…

Okay Doctor thanks. **Doctor Cuminme** please report to the emergency room for a phallic extraction.

Beep… beep… beep… (The heart monitor sound).

Ahhh… Mom! Mom! Yeah I'm here, I'm here Mom. What, what, what happened?

Jane I don't know! Heather and I were in this vagina bust in **Rio** and the next thing I knew was I was in the Medevac being flown out of the Sex-War zone. Baby, its door to door now, the fighting is rough. No condoms, no chastity belts, nothing. It's cunt to cunt combat! It's one hole at a time, one convert at a time! It's fuck-horrible!

BEEP, BEEP... BEEP...

Mom, your heart rates spiking! Just shut-up! And stop getting excited or you'll never recover.

Yeah Sandy, just calm down and tell me and Jane what really happened. We're gonna help you.

Oh Jane, Mary, me and Heather were literally working our asses off trying to use as much anal persuasion as we can to get these Latin American men on the salvation track. It's a fucking war!

Well calm down and tell us everything.

And wow! Are those Casanova types horny! And they're heads are as rock-hard as their erections! You tell them they can be saved by the worship of the one true God the Cock and that the Virgin Mother was a Vaganus®. Then everything went from bad to worst. The next thing we knew, I'm chocking, no literally drowning on sperm. Load after load!

Oh Mom! (Hugs and kisses).

Yeah, the Brazilians are heavy creamers! I was fine. Heather and I were putting out with our backdoor pussies for this really big gang. Who just kept teases us, bring us to orgasm after orgasm. They had us begging for their loads.

Mom! Tell me you were wearing protection?

Yes, yes, **Jane**, me and **Heather** both had our government issued Chastity-Belts® on, the really sexy pink ones with the rear entry back. You know we're trained for this kinda stuff. And then, it just escalated into an all-out fuckfest Fuck-Out, **FO** [7.G1.6] party.

Holy-Poop! They can't treat you like that! It's against the Geneva Cum-vention [7.G1.7d]. You were emotionally wounded!

Wow a non-regulated FO in the middle of a Sex-War zone. It's barbaric!

Yeah, no proctor or proctologist, no support personal, nothing! Jane there had to be thousands of dicks in us!

Beep... beep... beep...

Okay Mom, just calm down, your vitals are stable now and they're gonna release you to me tomorrow. I want you to cum home to my place here in DC to recover.

Oooh Jane! You know your Mother's gotta get back in the field! I got Church work to do.

NO! Sniff, Sniff... NO YOUR NOT! Sniff, Sniff... You're cuming home with me and resting. Don't start talking silly things about saving the world! Doctor Cuminme told me you have anal pussy fatigue. One more orgasm and it would have been lights out! Click! (Jane snaps her fingers). Anal fatigue isn't a joke! It's a serious condition.

Anal what? Cum-on! I gotta get back in the action!

Anal fatigue. It's when you take it up the ass too much! And you need a break Mom. You're working yourself into a grave! Kiss, I love you. And besides Mary and I have some HCC stuff to discuss with you and Heather, so its break time. That's an order!

Wow Jane, aren't you the boss! (Sandy says mockingly).

Well yeah! You're the boss at home Mom, but as a Free-Pimped Whore, an **FPW** [8.H3.14] I do out rank you in the Church.

[5.9] MOMMIES

There, you comfortable Mom?

Oh **Jane**, I love you sweetheart. Mwah… You've helped me and Heather so much. (Sandy hugs her daughter).

Mom, I want you to have the best.

Me too **Sandy**. (Mary chimes in). I want you and Heather to be happy.

Ahh… Mary, Jane, I love you Gurls. Me and Heather couldn't have had better kids then you two! And we're happy. Mwah… (Sandy and Heather embrace).

Hey Mom, Sandy, there's something Jane and I need to talk to you guys about.

Yeah, Jane said something at the hospital about you wanting to talk to us.

So, what's so important you couldn't WeeChat me about?

Ohhhh… Don't you dare tell me you and Mary are going to adopt one of those Sissy Babies from the farm! I won't have it!

No, no, no… You're right, it would be crazy. Okay, here it is, Jane and I have received a Sissy breeding notice from the SBP.

Okay, great! When do we get to meet the lucky human breeding gals you shack-up with? I hope there knockout gorgeous! You two deserve the best.

Ahhh…. Well Moms. Ahhh…. How do I say this? It's funny, we've known about this breeding notice for a while and I've spent hours and days thinking about how to tell this to you guys.

Mary! Sweetheart, spit it out already!

What the heck are you babbling about?

Okay! Sniff, Sniff… (Mary is having a little meltdown). Jane and I are knocking you guys up! There! I said it.

Ahhhhhh… !!!…

Mary! Where's she going? Mary! Cum back Sweetheart (Beth shouts at Mary who scampers off to the kitchen in tears). Mary!

Hang-on. I'll go talk to her. Mary! Mare! (Jane goes in pursuit).

Sniff, sniff, sniff…

Mare hey! (Jane fines Mary in the bedroom crying, hugs her). We're in this together. We'll see this through to the end.

Sniff, sniff... Okay Jane. Your kid, our kids are my step-Sissy-daughter, step-Sissy-Sister-in-law, Sissy-daughter-aunt, how the hell do you figure I can deal with this? Ahhh... Sorry, I just process this whole thing differently.

They'll be the children we both love, plain and simple. (Jane asserts some logic into a somewhat illogical family tree).

Sniff... Sniff... Sure Jane, one big incestuous fuck-monkey gang! We're only a Sissy-Family®. We don't know whose kid is whose! We have crazy lives! We're just Government own Sex-Toy® products. How do we deal with this Jane. Mwah...

Mwah... Hey, stop worrying. And Mare I really don't know what the universe has planned for us. Honey, I just try to see the harmony in things. Mwah... Be at peace with everyone. Kiss kisss... I've been reading about Lao-Tzu and Eastern Philosophy lately. The **Tao Pee Ching** [24]. And I think everything has a purpose. It will all be fine.

> *A journey of a thousand kilometers*
> *must begin with a single step*

Oooh, cum on Jane! Don't be going all Zen on me now!

Hey! We'll do this journey together Mare. Let's go back out there (Jane has her arm around Mary's shoulder). Me & you buddy. Kiss. I love you. Mwah...

Back with the moms...

Hey, sorry about the melt-down, sniff, sniff... Mwah...

Don't be Mary. Mwah… We're actually a little stunned by what we think you just told us. Explain it to us.

Just don't blame me and Jane Okay? This is just what the Sissy Breeding Program, the **SBP** [4.D-G6.2] instructed us to do. Mwah…

Honey! Huh, many years ago Sandy and I were instructed to do an equally as shocking procedure.

Yeah we know all about the bonding procedure Mom.

You know about it?

Mom me and Jane are Branded Whores, it's the highest rank for a Sissy in Sissydom. We know a lot of stuff. But this mating with each other's mom, is a little too much for me.

Honey, sometimes you just gotta role with it. Mwah…

Huh sure, I, we, us, all love each other, so yeah! I'm in. Here are the instructions, Mom, Jane is your husband and I'm Sandy's.

The **SBP** will be sending you instructions via WeeeChat for the inoculation.

Okay, when is this going to go down?

Well we first have to submit the marriage applications. Then you breeders have to report for inoculation prep. And then we have the marriage ceremony, and…

Oh yeah, well me and Heather have done the whole breeding preparation thing before. Easy-peasy!

Okay then finally after you ladies have been prepared for impregnation, we do the deed.

The deed?

Yeah the deed, you know, Jane and I jump your bones, knock you up, sowing our seeds, bun in the oven.

Oh! Yeah, well we've all been making love forever, it's just we change which hole and the result. I'm fine.

Yeah Mom, basically this time you don't take it up the ass, we're gonna do it in your baby makers!

Thanks for that graphic explanation sweetheart! Mwah… Relax Mary. Everything will turn out fine. Mwah…

Heee hee, haaa, haaa Ahhh... (All four of them hug and toss round). Kissss… Cum here! One big family hug (They're all feeling each other up & making out). Kiss… Mwah…

[5.10] BYE MOMS

Several days later…

Yes Mom I'll call you, we're only going to Germany and then on to India to deliver **ASB** [4.D-G3.12]. Nothing to dramatic.

Hey we love you both (Heather and Sandy have their arms around each other they're obviously in love as their tongue dance with each other). Hmmm… Kisss...

Mom! Get a room! Do you have to do the Lesbian making-out thing in from us!

Jane! Cum-on! Like you don't make-out with girls?

Okay! Yeah, but they're not my Mother and or Wife.

Hey look at the time! We gotta catch this plane. Bye Moms, try not to get into trouble. And contact the **SBP** [18.7.2] about the special inoculation preparation.

Huh! I'm your Mother! I'm supposed to be the one telling you what to do!

Well cum to the MSES, you just got demoted to our wives, so enjoy your new role in life, listening to us bitch and moan at you.

That's not fair!

Gotta go! See you when we get back from **India**! Kiss... (Hugs and kisses).

Chapter 6: EURASIA

[6.1] VODKA

Oh **Cardinal Popoff** it's so good to meet you again. Mwah…

Mwah… Oooh Mary, likewise and under better circumstances this time.

Haa haaa… Yeah! No abductions I hope.

Haaa, haa… Yes, just a nice friendly chat about what's be cuming a very hot cum-modity in the world markets. And in Berlin, it is such a beautiful city.

Yes, Berlin is beautiful. And it is still illegal for Sissies to enter into Russia so we needed to meet here. How did you manage to get a visa into Germany?

Oh! Huh, Jane and I are registered as farm animals with special attributes. So, we're here to be studied by some zoologists.

That's great! They're going to study your big beautiful boobs I hope as I do. They are a magnificent pair, Mary.

Ahhh… No! But your hands feel good on them. Ahhh… No there're plenty of big breasted women in Germany. More like they're going to pull out their big Germanic pricks and probe us. But hey! I love a good probing and its Jane's favorite thing to do. We're making a whole spa day out of it. With the scientists, massages, hot tub and of course a lot of probing our special attributes. Very scientific! (Mary winks). Haa… haaa...

Very! Good! I'm glad you Gurls are going to enjoy yourselves here in Germany.

Cardinal getting back to the installation plan, we're estimating full ad-Dick-tion by the year 2300.

Well its 2254 now, so you estimate in 46 years. In Moscow we came up with more optimistic figures. We predict total saturation of the Vaganus market by 2256.

Wow! Ahhh... I'll have my statistician's contact your statistician's. And **Popoff,** you realize statistics only tell you what you massage data to tell you! I mean, back home in the USA Inc. our government keeps tell folks there's no unemployment.

Yes, but the American government always bullshits about things to keep the angry mob from storming the Whitehouse gates.

Right Popoff! Mwah... I'm glad you understand. Everyone is unemployed because they're working three jobs for minimum wage or just fell-off the grid.

This is a very misfortunate thing and my condolences to you and your once great nation. But Mary, this whole ad-Dick-tion program will move rapidly if you can supply the personal and equipment.

Yes, yes... Cardinal we have the Doctors-without-Booty [23.39] and nurses. Most of them are Russians who secretly practice Cockolicism here in Russia.

Wow! Excellent Mary, Aghhh... Yes! **Jane**! Just like that sweetheart. Oooh... She's good! Jane you are the best! Ahhh...

Cardinal she's my Bitch! She better be good. I trained her myself. (Mary states in a confident, matter-of-fact tone).

Well in that case **Mary**, do you have other Bitches you could sell me?

Cardinal Popoff! Huh! No! I'm a one Bitch kind of DOM.

Okay, okay... Sorry, I find this to be surprising. Most DOM Ladies your age and statue have several large harems. Well! Not important, I have an entire Nunnery of Sissies at the Vaticum to choose from. So Mary, you chose Kiev as a starting point?

Well yeah! The **Ukame** [25.36a] is a great place to launch this type of enterprise from. The Americans setup there many, many years ago. The USA Inc. infiltrated into most non-Nuclear Cunt-tries first with an NGO like the National Emasculation for Democracy, the **NED** [25.33]. Then they start a coup which leads to crimes against humanity, all in the guise of democracy.

Yes, yes... The American government is like a maggot! Constantly looking to profit from other nations by putting themselves where they don't belong.

True Cardinal, I'm ashamed of what my Cunt-trie has done to others. The USA Inc. has 690 military bases around the world just so they can spread the ad-Dick-tion to Vaganus and turn a profit. Snifff... Snifff... (Mary fights back some tears).

There, there Mary. Times are changing!

Dominance through ad-Dick-tion!

Yes! Change is good! Huh! (Mary sighs). But, it makes me sad to think of the suffering it caused. But enough of this horrible past history, let's focus on Kiev!

Yes, yes… Kiev is a great place to setup the installation groups and or a sexual revolution. The Ukame is close to Europe. And reinstated as a Russian state due to war reparation makes it a perfect place to smuggle in the **SSAAAS** equipment [4.D-G1.26]!

Oooh! And about tomorrow in India, your contact **Rahul** (EN10) has been working closely with the Church on implementation of the, One-Cock World-Order Initiative, the **OCWO** [9.B.1]. So everything will work perfectly for you and the American Sissy Babies, the **ASB**® [4.D-G3.12] you're delivering.

Great Cardinal! Mwah… Thank you for setting up the connection in India.

Of course Mary! And Mary, don't forget, us Russians are hung like horses, we'll never be able to produce the kind of high quality Sissies you do back in America. So Mwah… Keep breeding more of those cute little darlings.

So Popoff, you're saying there'll always be a perpetual market for ASB® here?

Da, Da! The Sissy Babies, the ASB® is the new American armed forces. And Mary, war is a very profitable business! The more of these little farm raised fuck-monkeys we proliferate the world with, the more money the Church and America makes! Now we drink! Vodka!

Ahhh… Cardinal **Popoff** I'm not a real heavy drinker, are you trying to take advantage of us?

Haa… Haaa… Of course I am! (Popoff grabs Mary's ass and is slobbering all over her like a drunken lush) Mwah… Ummm… (Mary tries to push away). Oooh cum on Mary! Kiss me! You can't conclude a Russian business deal without drinking vodka! And having lots of sex!

Nostrovia… !!!...

Well okay if you insist! Jane, stop milking for a moment and cum-up and out from under the table. Baby, please drink with me and our lustful Cardinal friend.

Okay, to the future of the Russian Orthodox Cockolic Church, Sissydom® and to Mother Russia. Nostrovia! Nostrovia! (And the drinking went on, and on into the wee hours).

The next afternoon….

Okay, Uooogh…. Uoooo… My head… Jane?

Yeah, I'm here Mare! (Jane shouts from lounge chair where she's reading an epic novel, the Rise and Fall of the American Penis).

Okay! Ummm… The Cardinal?

She left earlier!

It was weird. Last night I woke up and she was banging away at my cunt while I thought she was saying something about me taking over the HCC position of *Mother Superior* of all the Nuns in the Church.

Wow! Juicy action. I was conked-out. Missed the whole thing.

Tssss... Whatever! Then I felt her pull out of me. But I fell back to sleep.

Here's a coffee. Popoff Jizzie creamed it for you.

Ahh! Thanks Baby. Sip, sip... Ooooh! This tastes sooo good. Ouch! My head hurts. You okay?

I'm okay, a little dizzy from last night. I've been up for hours. I gave her a nice long BJ and swallowed her load for breakfast. Then she strapped her flaccid FEM-Cock® to her thigh and left for Church to give Cum-fessions.

Cool! Kisss... Kisss. (Jane jump back on the bed and crawls into Mary's arms). Cardinal **Popoff** is really something else. Quite a sumptuous and sensuous Lady.

Yeah, yeah... Beautiful Lady. I really like her. Kiss... Mwah... I had my head between her legs all night. Wow! I can still taste her sweet pussy in my mouth. Ummm.... Let's cum to Russia more often!

Jane! Huh! (Mary is holding her head and sighs).

Yeah Lover? Mwah... Cum-on! Wake-up sleepy head!

Jane, what are we doing? (Mary blurts out an open-ended question).

Ahhh... Okay now you're scaring me. Drink your coffee, wake-up! Mwah... Cum-on! Wake-up! (Jane is always bubbly and cheerful, full of energy).

No, no… I mean, the vodka, the salvation missions to jungles, distributing babies, Cockolicism, our President is a douche-bag, the Sissy Army, Whoring Stations, FEMA camps. What are we doing **Jane**?

Whoa, whoa, whoa… Mare! You know what it is. We've discussed this many, many times. Don't go off into one of your philosophical rants.

What, what, what's our mission in life, Jane? Where's all this going if anywhere? (Mary is just over-cum by the complexity of their lives).

Mary, it's the vodka talking.

Jane! I'm confused. (Mary is a wreck from the night before and has a puzzled look on her face).

Mare! Look at me! We've been over this stuff a 69 million times. It's Sissydom! There is no explanation! We're pawns on a game board and we're just playing the game! End of story! We're Switzerland! Neutral participants.

Are we? Are we doing what's right Jane? Are we bad people? Geopolitical intervention, profiting from death. Is this what America is all about?

Mare, Mare… Honey, its moments like this that make me want to love you even more. Mwah… Look! You're lucid and you're not sounding crazy. Yes! We work for an evil Empire! But that's not us! We're Bonobo Gurls, we believe in love and peace and harmony. We're good people, Mare.

Jane (Mary sighs). I'm I gonna be able to do this? Am I strong enough? There're so many people depending on me!

Hey, hey… Let's just say this. The powers in control, truly believe you're all in. As long as you fool the military Joint Chiefs of **Shafts** [25.12.1], the douche-bag in the Whitehouse and Cockolic Church, everything is fine! Mare, you are a great player, a political artist. You can totally fool them!

Am I Jane? Or am I just fooling myself?

Huh! Drink your Jizzed coffee and chill out. Mwah… And hey! Do you seriously think things are going to stay the same? Mare, you know they won't. Things change, whatever happens, we'll just play the game! The rules will change, but we'll always be together, playing whatever game the big wealthy Stud-Boys cum up with. Kisss...

Kisss…. Hug me Sweetheart. (Mary says as Jane, being much smaller than Mary, drapes herself over her true love). Mwah…

Mwah… I'll always be here for you Mare.

[6.2] INDIA

In India the erotic subcontinent…

Hey! So how did we end up in New Delhi?

Jamitin and **Popoff** turned us on to this connection. **Rahul** is high up on the pecking order around here, so he can do a lot of off-the-books stuff.

It's warm here! (Jane smirks).

Jane, I thought you'd be happy to be in such an exotic place? The Kama Sutra, the sex positions. This is a great place for sex lovers like you. Where's your sexual desires today?

At the bottom of a Vodka bottle! Ouch! My head still hurts.

Well yeah! But Geeez... There are lots and lots of people here! Haa haaa... More people to be practicing sex positions with! Haaaa... (Mary picks up and hugs her tiny little side-kick). Mwah...

Mwah... Very funny, not! Wow! The Eunuchs are doing public bow-jobs, **PBJ** [4.D-G2.14] in the street. Cool! Now that's Cock-Sucking talent! Huh! Very talented! And they really have no balls, awesome! Look they're very traditional all dressed-up in colorful saris garb.

Ah yes, the eunuch, the Third-Sex. Cum on Jane! Stop gaping at the Eunuchs missing parts. Look, there's Rahul. Rahul! Over here!

Ahhhh... Ms. Dune! Well cum to India! Mwah... Mwah...

Thank you **Rahul**! Good to meet you.

Ahhh... How are you? You must be Jane? Mwah...

Mwah... Yes, I'm Jane. Good to meet you.

How was your trip?

Great! Wow! Rahul it sure is crowded here in India!

Yes, yes... There are a lot of people here in India and the over population of the Eunuchs is a problem.

Well **Rahul**, thanks for getting us in the Cunt-tree on the livestock visa for the wink, wink, experimental test. Very clever ploy on your part.

Oooh sure! I hope you and Jane won't mind going to the animal control center for the actual experiment.

No, no… Absolutely not. We don't mind at all. It's always the same procedure. We'll start in a lab as an experiment and it ends up be cuming, let's share the love moment fuckfest. And hey! Jane and I love a good probing! Haaa haa…

To be continued….

[6.3] EXOTIC

So **Rahul**, Jamitin tells me you're onboard with this?

Oooh Ms. **Dune**, our sect of the **CI** here in India is probably the most erotic group you will ever meet. When this plan was put up for a vote to the **Grand Masters**, it passed unanimously. But Ms. Dune, you realize… (Mary interrupts).

Please Rahul call me Mary.

Ahhhh… Yes, of course especial under these sir-Cum-stances, (He has his hands up Mary's skirt) Ahh… Mary you realize the whole sexual nature of your plan with the introduction of the Bonobo Sissy Gurls is fine with the laws and culture here in India. After all this is the Exotic Subcontinent. We invented eroticism!

Oooh sure, **Rahul**. Our Gurls will blend right in here.

Yes! But it will be illegal to perform the installation of the payment equipment in open view of the Indian government?

Yes, yes... Rahul we have the medical professionals you need to pull this off, Agh! Many of them are from India and are already ad-Dick-ted to the Vaganus®.

Yes Mary, it is good we have the personal needed here. Yes, suck me off now, Agh! Ahhh... Yes... Ohhh... You're a nice Sissy Lady Mary. Hmmm... Thank you.

Mwah... Thank you Rahul. I was actually hungry. And Rahul, Hmmm... (Mary licks her lips). You taste yummy. Kiss...

Kiss... So we'll deliver the babies to the hospital or clinic. Then the adopting family members prior to the physical delivery are examined and the **PDE**® [4.D-G1.14] installation is performed?

Exactly! This way the system has, unbeknownst to the parents, a fully functional participating family in the Indian MSES, or IN-MSES.

[6.4] BENEFITS

Employer's with benefits deal...

Rahul how are we going to win the cooperation of the employers to use the LCT payment system?

Oh please **Mary**! We have all of this arranged. The local Cock-illuminati, the **CI**® [9.A.1] is working closely with the Labor Ministry to compensate through a phone app. Besides this is the year 2254, most employers nowadays use electronic transfer to pay workers. And once inside the digital world, where and when the compensation happens is very hard to trace. It is be cuming part of the shadow economy.

Mary we're adapting the HOMO, Section 12, Appendix L of the SM069 manual [12.L1.9].

Male Orgasm (MO)
Pay Rank (PR)
Pay Per Hour in cents (PPH)
Dollar(s) Per MO in dollars (DPM)

Yes, **Rahul**, I got all of your correspondence. What I'm not clear about is the why the employer would bother changing pay systems?

Mary, it's simple. The employer gets free Sissy booty for the rest of their lives!

Okay. And if they don't cooperate?

Huh! We castrate them! Problem solved!

Wow! Rahul! You **CI**® guys don't mess around!

Shhhh…it No! When it cums to matters of the **Sex-Soul** [21.B.24.2], love and the spiritual world, India is the center of the universe!

Wow! Okay Rahul, let me get this straight. If they do not cooperate you turn them into Eunuchs?

Yes! And Mary, our universe is expanding. India is part of the EAU the Eurasian Union and we have a lot of laborers at sites up on Mars. They are constructing replicas of Indian Temples of Sex as new World Heritage sites. All of those workers need compensation of an erotic nature, if you know what I mean?

Yep! Mwah… Sissy-Puss!

Right! And the Temples will need to be staffed by Eunuchs or Sissies either or would do. But the Eunuchs will be in short supply since India passed a law against castration unless you commit a major crime.

Awesome Rahul! We have the Bitches you need! And they're not castrated. Mwah…

Mwah… Yeah they just have tiny little nut-snacks like you & Jane. Mwah… You Gurls are sooo cute! Mwah…

Heee… hee… Great! Glad you like us Gurls. Mwah…

We need all the Sissies you can supply us Mary. At least 69 thousand! Maybe more!

No problem Rahul! (Mary agrees knowing it will be next to impossible to supply the volume Rahul is talking about).

Mary, you know I'm ad-Dick-ted right? Haahaa… Obviously! You been poking me with your boner since we met!

Oooh Mary! You are a temptress. Fact is, all of the **CI**® here in India is ad-Dick-ted to making love to Sissy Gurls. We've all converted over to Sissydom® and defend the new moral convictions of **Cockolicism**®.

Yeah, you mentioned it several times with a suggestive tone. And you know, we embrace the opportunity of making love with men from the mysterious exotic subcontinent. Mwah…

Well then! You and Jane will be our guests at my home! My wife **Priya** (EN10) and I insist you spend your time in India being pampered by my family!

Sure Rahul, it's so kind of you to invite us into your home. Kiss, Kiss... Hmm... (His hands are down her blouse and panties). Mwah...

Delivering the ASB the next day...

Wow, this is quite a lavish place, the owners must be wealthy.

Yes, all the CI families we're visiting are. And in recent years the multi-wife laws have been re-written to accommodate as many wives as is desired by the man of the house. So you will typically see an enormous estate which is separated out into several households. For example this man Mahesh has ten families. So we're delivering ten ASB® to him and his ten wives.

Whoa! Rahul, who the hell is going to supply the baby food if there's only one Daddy?

Oh cum on Mary! This is India, there're over five billion people in this country! Don't you worry your pretty little head over silly matters like this! Okay. There are plenty of cum hoses around to fulfill the demand for Sissy food. Ah here's Mahesh...

Mahesh! My brother!

Ah Rahul, and I see you've brought the American temptresses with you! Ah! Welcum to my home, I'm Mahesh (Mahesh kisses both Jane and Mary, his huge erect penis is sticking out of his exotic looking robe).

Mary Rahul has told me so many things about you and Jane. Your adventures, intimate moments, the Church, politics. You're my kind of lady, sexy, smart, and ambitious! Move to India, be one of my wives!

Haa… Haaa… Mahesh I'm flattered, but I'm married to a wonderful wife and I'm afraid my life and work does not allow me the time to be a housewife for you or any man.

Well, you can't blame a man for trying.

Ahh… It feels good, hmmm… Mahesh, let's becum intimate later, first we need to get the Babies to their new Mothers and train the family members and staff on how to handle a Sissy child, whoops! I mean an infant baby.

The ABS is delivered to the Mothers…

There you go, that's fine and the baby formula is unique for these babies so do not substitute it with dairy milk or baby formulas. Rahul, how many of these mothers know the POOP babies are not really human?

Oh Mary, it's a IN-CI family, all of them know the ASB feed on cock milk. Like I said, stop worrying.

They know they're Sissies. And believe me Mary, this country has been dealing with sexuality things like Sissies for thousands of years. It always amazes me to realize most of you Westerners, especially American's have zero experience or knowledge in the erotic nature of India. Humans have been screwing each other and animals in any hole available since the beginning of time.

You gotta point there Rahul.

Yes, and are religious rules and government laws going to stop Sissydom or Homosexuals or Lesbians, Vagina, Cock & Vaganus® worship or whatever? NO! People need to do what makes them happy and if this happens, the world would be a better place!

So true Rahul, so true. Kiss… You're a real worldly man Rahul. Thanks Kisss…

Hours later…

Okay, the Babies look happy.

Yes Mary they will be well loved here in this peaceful place. Ahh… you see they suckle the penis like a mothers tit nipple. Ahh what a happy little Sissy baby.

Mary you Sissies are so, human looking yet so different than us Homo sapiens. Yes Mahesh we, the Homo-Sis-Sapiens are loving, kind and very sensual creatures. Mary, as an Indian man from the most erotic point on the global, I think this sounds odd coming from a Western person, but you and Jane are a different type of Westerner. Please share with me the Sissy art of lovemaking? I wish to experience what I've heard so much about. I want to be as loving as a Sissy.

Surely Mahesh, it would be our pleasure to share with a human man who actually thinks of us as more than just barnyard animals and as the loving creatures we are.

My wives and Rahul will all be joining us… Kiss… Kiss…

The next morning…

You two please cum again! Our home is yours. Kiss… Kiss…

Yes, we will, it was a night we will never forget. Kiss… Kiss… Take care of the Babies, share their love making with everyone!

We will, there will be so many Vaganus® lovers here on the Sub-Continent of India. Good Bye to all of you, I love you... Kiss... Kiss... Kiss...

That my friends Mary is what India is all about, love, peaceful times and lots of sex!

Hey Rahul it was great. And yeah, men are hang like horses here!

Haa haaa... Jane! Yeah this is your kind of place Baby.

And Uniks are cool too...

Haaa... Haa... Jane you please easy!

One week later, good bye....

Rahul this was only the first batch of **ASB®** with many more to cum. Thank you for helping us with the distribution.

Yes of course! But Mary, we will need so many more American Babies (wink, wink) of the **B-Type** [1.A2.2] kind if you know what I mean?

Yes, yes... We'll send you plenty of little Bitches. Kiss... And Rahul, you'll report to me on a weekly basis won't you? Mwah... (Mary sucks up to Rahul to gain his support).

Yes, Yes... Absolutely Mary. And we will miss you and Jane very much. Kisss, kiss... Let us know when you have the Mars supply order ready.

Yes Rahul, we'll prepare the contract for your approval. But first we have a couple of weddings to go to.

And Mary, don't forget. We need them, young, eager and trained! Got it? See you soon. Mwah…

Chapter 7: Mommy Time

[7.1] BREEDING

September and the FEM Breeding wedding…

We're back! Ahhh… Dear Lord! (As the Gurls simultaneously plop onto the sofa).

Huh! What a trip! **Mare**, did you call the Moms?

Yeah I called them. And no more Vodka!

Haaa Haa… It was a hell of a goodtime! Great people. I gotta feel we'll be going on a lot of these kinda trips.

Did we really do the entire Russian Assembly?

Yeah we drained their balls, all 620 of them.

Wait that would be 1240 balls!

Haa haaa… Yes Jane, in total balls drained. Haa haaa… Oooh Jane, I love you so much. Kiss. Mwah…

Mwah… Mare at this rate, you know you'll make Generals rank some day in the Army Sissy Reserve.

Yeah maybe, so what!

And you're the **Mother Superior** now. You're gonna make all this work, Sissydom, Politics, Church now fame! Everybody loves Mary.

Hey! I hear what you're saying Jane and how you're saying it. Listen Baby, I don't care if they blame it on me, fame it on me, we're both taking the credit. Kiss... Kisss... Cum here you! (Mary hugs Jane tight) Do you think for a minute you're gonna be able to slip away from me, you little Sissy Bitch. Hmmm... Jane, me & you sweetheart. Kiss... Mwah...

Mwah... Love you Mary.

Love you too. I can't do this without you Sugar-Puss! Now we have to start working on the wedding stuff. I put in for our vacation time. So we're free! Yah!

Yeah Mare, now all we have to do is knock-up each other's Mom. (Jane gives a questioning smirk to Mary). Huh! I can't believe we're doing this!

[7.2] MARRIAGE

The Gurls marry the other ones mom...

Huh! I can't believe we're getting Breeding married! Honey, please pass me my butt plug.

Why?

Jane, I don't want to poop on my nice wedding dress. The Sissy groom shouldn't be all poopied-up when she meets her wife at the Altar.

Dresses! Agh! There're so cumfining!

Jane! Put it on and leave it on, don't embarrass us at the wedding. (Parental Mary says).

Hey! I've been in a dress ever since we got to Washingcum. You know this is torture for me.

Haa haaa… Tsss… Jane. you call a mini-skirt a dress. You're so funny Jane.

Hey I'm trying to impress your political cronies, friend or foe.

Oh! Look what time it is. Agh! Hurry up we gotta go! We can't be late for our own weddings.

At the hometown HCC parish Church…

Dearly beloved we are gathered here today in the sight of our God the almighty Cock. And in the presence of these Cock worshipping witnesses to join together these couples entering into the Sacred Holy bond of Sissy Breeding matrimony.

Since it is your intention to enter into the covenant of matrimony, join your right hands, and declare your consent before the Cock our God and the Church.

I Sissy **Jane**, take you, Human **Heather**, to be my Sissy breeding wife. I promise to satisfy your sexual needs in good times and in health. I will love you and honor your needs to breed Sissies all the days of my life.

I Human **Heather**, take you, Sissy **Jane**, to be my husband. I promise to breed faithfully with you in good times and in health, to love you and to honor your desire to breed Sissies with me all the days of my life prior to menopause.

I Sissy **Mary**, take you, Human **Sandy**, to be my Sissy breeding wife. I promise to satisfy your sexual needs in good times and in health. I will love you and honor your needs to breed Sissies all the days of my life.

I Human **Sandy**, take you, Sissy **Mary**, to be my husband. I promise to breed faithfully with you in good times and in health, to love you and to honor your desire to breed Sissies with me all the days of my life prior to menopause.

You my kiss the brides... Kiss... Kiss... Kisss... Kiss

Oh I can't believe we're all married to each other and I have no idea what to call our children.

But they're going to be FEMs so we gotta cum up with Gurl names.

Well there's a 69 percent chance of them being FEMs.

Right they inoculated us with the **F-Type** formula, so I'm hoping for a FEM baby.

Ahhhh... **Father Tom**! Thank you for performing the ceremony.

Oh! It's my pleasure. Mwah... Here you two are, I could remember giving you First Holy Cum-Union when you were babies. Now look at you!

Mwah... Good to see you too father Tom.

I've been reading the HCC newspaper articles about you two. I'm so proud of you both. And you being from this Parish has made us somewhat famous amongst the faithful.

Huh! Famous Father?

Oh yeah! They even started a fund drive to build a monument of the two of you!

Holy-Cock! (Mary & Jane look at each other in shock)

Oh! And there's word the Pope is going to make the, Blessed Sissy Lady of Cock-Whores Church a Sacred Shrine because of the work the two of you have done to spread Sissydom® throughout the world! I can see in now, tour buses and a Mary & Jane Annual Sissy Festivals and…

Father Tom!

Yes Sister Martha! (The Nun whispers in Father's ear as he grabs her ass).

Oh! Well spank the little Sissy on the ass a few times she'll suck on it! Geeez... Some of these new Sissies are dumb as a Non-Stud. You gotta jump-start them into having sex. Huh! But not you two! (Father points at the Gurls). You two were horny from birth, no encouragement needed.

Father! We need you. Mwah… (The Nuns call out seductively for Father Tom while tweaking their nipples at him).

Okay Cuming! Duty calls. See you Gurls later! I'll cream-fill you during the grand-exit! Oh and please do send me the video of the Consummation & Conception of your Sissy babies.

We will Father Tom! Mwah… huuh1 He's still a horn-dog after all these years.

Cocktails, dancing, toasts, speeches, dinner, cake, garter & bouquet toss, mother & groom and father & bride penetration, BJs, photos and the grand exit, on to the honeymoon suite…

Ahhhh… Our Honeymoon suite.

Wow! And you said Rimme and Yaoi are paying for the whole wedding?

Huh! Rimme and Yaoi must like you Gurls a whole lot!

Mom, you know as a Nun I service Rimme, right? But we haven't told you the other things we are to the Cardinals and the Church.

Hey! I don't need to know. You know how secretive the Church is. It's on a need to know basis.

Yeah this is my point. The HCC newspaper articles about us, they don't tell you what's really going on, they sugar-coat the stories.

So Mary what side of the story do you want me to believe?

Okay, all this lavishness is what I mean to Rimme. Wait, are you married to her? No, no… You can't marry a….

MARY! (Jane interrupts Mary from divulging Church secrets).

Oh yeah! Whoops! Maybe I had a few too many drinks at the reception. (Mary is sloshed). Hick-up! Hick-up!

Mare! Can I have a word with you? (Jane gets them away from the Moms). What the hell are you blabbing about out there to your Mother? You know we can't tell them about our Pimps and us being Branded Whores!

Jane they're gonna fine out in the end! Hick-up! Once we get in bed with them tonight and they see our Pimps serial numbers branded on our asses, they'll know we're **FPW** [2.B2.7]. Look I spoke to Rimme about it and she said now that we're married to them we can tell them anything. They have the right to know who we are.

Okay! Are you gonna tell mind or am I telling yours or....

Oh for the Love-of-Cock! Hick-up! Jane, I don't care who tells who! Ahhh!! Let's just enjoy this night sweetheart. Kiss... Kisss... Let's go make our FEM daughters.

Moms! Mary and I have to tell you something.

Oh Jane, we know you're both Pimped-Whores®.

Huh! How did you know?

Honey! We were briefed when we showed up for the FEM inoculation preparation. We've been at the Sissy Breeding Preparation facility for 6 weeks 9 days getting ready. They been pumping us up with the Sissification® cross-breeding F Formula, **SFF69** [4.D-G1.10] to get us ready to accept your foreign sperm into our human bodies. Its standard procedure to tell you all the information about who you're breeding with.

Huh! Okay, nothing to hide here. Hick-up! (Mary staggers over to the bed and prior to collapsing onto it, bends over and exposes the brand on her ass cheek). Hick-up!

Aaaah! Cute Sweetheart. (Heather says in passing while telling her story of the ordeal). Anyway, there also an HCC representative there and we signed a lot of documents about who owns who and who owns what and when and where and... Believe me, when they were done making us sign everything, we didn't know who owns what! Or who! Or... And I don't know or care who owns what anymore. They explained the whole thing about the Pimp Whore Partnership (PWP) rules and regulations.

Hey! Can we just go to bed now? Look we have our Bridal Lingerie on, isn't it turning you guys on? Mwah…

Haa ha haaa… Yeah, Sandy it is, I have a tiny little boner for you. Kiss… Mwah…

Jane it's bedtime? (Heather informs her Breeding husband).

Yes Heather my lovely Breeding wife. Hmmm… I'm a wife doing a wife. This is kinda weird!

Oooh and look at the time, we need to perform the Consummation on or before midnight. Places everyone!

[7.3] BREEDING FEMS

The Consummation & Conception…

Yeah, yeah… Stop reading the breeding instruction manual and put it in Mary! You're hard, just stick it in! (Sandy just wants to make love to Mary as she has done so many times in the past). Kisss… Kisss… Ummm… Yeah…

Sandy, I've never been in you baby-maker, your pussy. Mwah…

Mwah… Mary, this is so natural to us. Mwah… We've all made love to each other so many times before! Agh! How sweet this is all of us together again in one bed, all of us copulating making babies. Oooh, it's nice. Mwah…

Ooooh! **Jane** Gurl. Mwah… (Heather whispers). Oooh! Shoot your seed in me my dear sexy breeding husband! Aghhh…. Yes, Hmmm… Now I'm happy! Kiss… Kiss… Mwah…

Oooh! Yeah… Yeah… Gimme your baby making cream **Mary**! Agh! I wanna have your Sissy Baby! Oooh! I wanna have my daughters Sissy husbands FEM child. Agh! Yes! Cum! Cum in me! Agh! Mwah…

The morning after…

Ahh… The coffee is sooo good.

Oh wow! The room service brought all this up for us? It's too much. Frapa-Cuma-Poop-Uccino.

Ahhh… I love this hotel. The **Whore-dorf** [3.C1.c.7] is just exquisite! The phallic statues, the erect shafts of the staff. They have Human and Sissy food, very nice. Yeah, wow they even have eggs, I haven't seen eggs in years.

Yeah, the animal food isn't around anymore.

Well there's what, 69 billion people on the planet earth now? There's just not enough food to feed the livestock animals and people too. Plus the Nitrous Oxide frats of the livestock was destroying the atmosphere.

Thank you Professor Mary! Kiss… Haa haaa…

Oh! And hey Gurls, we knew about the Brands years ago, we didn't know who gave them to you or what they meant. But you guys would have cum to us if you were in trouble. We didn't raise dumb kids.

No you didn't. Kiss… And we did what we thought was smart at the time. It turned out to be the best decisions of your lives thanks to the guidance you showed us when we were little. We knew how to survive. Kiss…

Kiss… So what's your next adventure?

Ahhhh… Huh! Mom my life is so complicated now. The Orthodox Cardinal told me on our trip, I would be taking over the HCC position of *Mother Superior* of all the Nuns in the Church. And I would be traveling to Rome several times a year to fulfill my obligation.

Wow! It's fantastic Honey! Congratulation! Kiss… Kiss...

Yeah, I'm honored and everything but where am I gonna find the time to do all this stuff? Do I quit the Directors position for the Church? Ahhhh… I'm just so confused! And I just got a WeeChat the other day from the Vatican asking me to cum in to assume the position.

It sounds very intimate to me! When do we go?

Jane, calm down. I have sooo much shhh…it happening it makes me dizzy.

Moms, where are you guys off to?

Oooh! We're going nowhere Honey. The SBP and HCC cancelled all our Missions of Salvation to Latin America. We can't leave the Cunt-tree pregnant because of the type of Sissy we're breeding. We're grounded! So it's keeping down the fort here for me, maybe read some erotica novels, I heard Sue Yan Nish is a good author.

And Dad? What's he up to?

Oh! You know your Dad. He's still doing her job at the C-Station. She's happy she takes his 269 loads a day, cums home tired, and watches some Fux news. Doesn't eat dinner because her belly is still full of Jizzzies from work.

Wait, what do mean her belly is full? Is she working a double load shift? She's taking it at both ends! Why Mom? You guys don't need the money and she's getting older, she shouldn't be work so hard! (Jane is upset about her dads work situation).

Honey, you know your Dad, she wants to take it for team. They were short staff at the Station so she's filling in. She's a real American patriot, volunteers at the Church, Cummunity Center Sissy-Fest events, donates to the Opt-Out Bonobo-Way fund to help the poor Non-Stud families transition into the Whore Class. I mean, your Dad's a really good Gurly boy.

Sniff... Sniff... That's my Dad! I love her so much. Sniff, Sniff... Oh Mom, Kisss... She'll be retired soon, so than you can spend a lot more time together.

Yeah, yeah... Hey, no tears, everything's fine.

Sniff... And the tribe?

Oh yeah! The wild Sissy tribe called our family. Ahhh... Sue (17 years old) your human sister is gonna graduate this year and she got accepted to FUCIT.

Awesome! Sue will make it to the top. She's smart.

Yeah, she wants to study Sissy Biology. She was thinking about whether to breed first and then go to school later like Heather did, but your Father was livid and forbid it. Hooo hoo… There were lots of arguments over that one.

And Mandy is starting high school and passed her **ASW**® exam, she's going to the same school you went to. Gonna do training in the same C-Station your Dad works at, just like you Jane. See you were the pioneer in this family! I'm so proud of you. Kiss.

Mom, Mary got me through all of it.

Oh! We're so lucky the two of you are a DOM-Bitch bonded pair, a **DBBP** [2.B2.13].

So is Mandy (13 years old) hooked-up with a DOM yet?

Funny you should ask, Jane. The SBP got in touch with me about her. It turns out there's a special program they want her to be part of.

Oh shhh…it Mom! Don't let them do anything dangerous to her!

Well I don't think it's that bad, Sweetheart. They were saying something about activating her dormant uterus. Something to do with inducing an existing reproductive organ.

Oh crap! Mom the government is always doing some shady weird experiments, test tubes, drugs, probing. All kinds of shhh…it!

Well I don't know. Mandy is so much like you Jane. She's bold and adventurous.

Huh! What about Sarah?

Oh, oh, oh… Sarah took the JSW exam early and passed it with the highest score. She's still in middle school and has the highest Cockage® score in her class! Just like you did Baby. Oh and I got her DOM match notice early from the SBP. So I'm pretty sure Sarah (12 years old) will be hooking-up with one of her classmates. I think her name is Susan Tampon.

Well what about you Heather? (Jane questions Mary's mom).

Same here. I'm grounded just like Sandy! But I'm enrolled in the Master degree program at Peniston University.

Wow! You're going back to school Mom? (Mary is startled by her mom's response).

Yeah Mare! I'm going all the way this time, gonna try for my Ph.D. I wanna be a Sissy Psychologist.

Mom! I love you! Agh! I'm so proud of you. Mwah…

And your Dad, she submitted her dissertation and when it's approved she'll have a PhD in Financial Vaganus Economics.

Ooooh! I'm so proud of you both. Mwah…

Yeah she's already got job offers as a financial analyst and might teach at Johns Hopkinky University.

[7.4] BYE MOM-WIVES

The Gurls are hitting the road again…

Okay so good luck with the *Mother Superior* position.

Yep! I'll let you know how it goes. If I survive the ceremony.

What do you mean ceremony?

Well Mom, you know the Church, with all their pomp and circumstance. And they weren't kidding about assuming the position. All the Cardinals have at me during the ceremony. And then I get to kiss the Popes Cock.

Wow Mare! So it should be quite an event! You actually get to kiss the pontiffs Holy-Cock. Wow…

Yeah and Jane is gonna be fluffing for me, so I'm sure there'll be some premature ejaculations! Haa haaa… Jane you Nymph! (Mary jokingly tries to grab Jane put she reacts so fast Mary seldomly catches her).

Hey! Call me when you know what's happening. (Heather says).

Yes Mom. Love you. Mwah…

You too Jane.

Yes, Heather my breeding wife. Kisss…

And Mary?

Yes, as soon as we know I'll WeeChat you.

Sandy my breeding wife (kisses & hugs goodbye) see you soon, stay out of trouble.

Me get into trouble? Hmmm… (Sandy stares with a naughty look).

Right Sandy, you and Jane are carbon copies of each other, why should I suspect you're gonna get into trouble? Haa haaaa... Hey but if you do cheat on me, at least send me a pic of his cock!

Mary Kiss. Hmm... (They're all hugging, feeling each other up, kissing goodbye) I Love you, kiss. Mwah....

Are you Gurls gonna be home for **Cock-Mas**?

Yes, Mom! You know us. We're always home on the holidays. But this holiday season we'll have so much more to celebrate. And Hey! Stop worrying. We're only going back to DC. I got a DHMC meeting.

Oh big things happening? (Heather asks)

Yes Snoopy Mom. Big stuff happening, but guess what? Nothing I can tell you about! Heee hee...

Well, I still love you, call me. Kisss. (Hugs and Kisses).

Okay talk soon. Mwah....

Chapter 8: Capitol Hill

[8.1] BUSTED

Back at the POOP office in Washingcum…

NOTICE: Free Pimped Whores, a **FPW**® [2.B2.7] must have permission from the Pimp who they are branded by to have Sissy-Sex with another Pimp. This infraction is in violation of your PIMP-WHORE Partnership, a **PWP**® [8] agreement and could lead to prosecution by said Pimp if so desired.

Busted you Whore! (Jane shouts at Mary).

Hey **Popoff** jumped me!

Hey I was there, don't lie to me! You were getting into it. And Mare I don't blame you, she's really hot, blonde bomb-shell of a FEM lady. Besides, we were on the road for three weeks without Pimp-Cream®. Sissies have needs!

Right Jane, this was an emergency situation. It's what I'll **WeeeChat** back to the LCT Violations Bureau. And I've already checked-in with Rimme about this, she said she would vouch for my excuse and the charges will be dropped.

You'll still have to pay the fine!

Nah! Assistant Director Goldberg your cousin is gonna pay it for me. Geeez… It was on State Department business. And seriously don't these guys understand, you gotta drain some balls to get anything done in this world!

[8.2] DHMC MEETING

The Latin America discussions continued...

Okay! Stop your hysterics! We have the Latin Americans! They're dependent on us for one if not more of the following things, money, drugs, Vaganus®, food, water. At this point we have 69 percent of Central and South America dependent on the USA Inc. for essential supplies. The Russians, sure they had a little foothold at first but we're in control now.

Okay Director **Dune**, well, what I'm making such a big fuss about is, we're pouring all our resources into the situation and seeing no return. Great we pump them up with opioid drugs like **SpermAid®** [14.O2.1], sexually reorient them and we get zero dollars back. So when are we going to see a profit?

Good question Senator **Cuming**. You're right! We can't just print money anymore like back in the Neocon-Fascist days! Now the United States Inc. has to actually make the Chinese money it spends. Too bad we can't convince China to screw the **Vaganus®** [14.O1.6] of an animal like we do here in America. But I digress.

In the case of Latin America, it has always cum down to what the USA Inc. can exploit out of them. And this is not always in the way of cash profit, it's typically resources.

Geeez... Jane this is a tough crowd (Mary whispers to Jane).

We're listening. Yes I agree, it's all about resources. In the past we used the Latin Americans as soldiers in the US Immigrant mercenary Army to invade Canada.

But we switched our military strategy from real boots on the ground with mercenary grunt soldiers to, dainty little Sissy Gurls in beds with lingerie and six inch pumps. I mean, if we were smart, we would use them in the same manner. Fight Sex-Battles with these Whores!

Wait a minute! I'm confused. What do you mean Director? I thought you told us they don't have small enough dicks to be transformed into American type Sissies?

Yes, yes… Latin Americans are useless as Sissies. Americans make the best Whores, hands down. For money or sex.

True Americans have always been the best Money-Whores or Sex-Whores. Look Dune, all I'm saying is maybe we set the bar to high.

Okay go on Dune. I'm cunt-fused about which Whore I prefer, however I do gravitate towards the Money-Whores because I have erectile problems. But go on. (Senator Mitch McCuntell says).

Well Sir. Americans tend to do this, we expect everybody in the world to have our standard. To do everything like us, for us. And this is a little optimistic and arrogant as well.

Dune! Everybody wants to be American! We have the right to be arrogant!

Ahhh…. You mean we used to. For example, my wife's Dad **Sam**, has been busting his **SIT**® [1.A2.4] ass as a common Hoe working in a **C-Station** [7.G4.C] all of his Transitioned Sissy life. And yeah! She chose to be a human transitioned to Sissy. She can't infect anyone like a real Sissy can because she's not actually a Homo-Sis-Sapien [18.3]. But this is how the whole

MSES® (EN01) started years ago. It started with whoever we could stick a dress on and then it progressed into the thriving, utopian system of today!

Director Dune, so what you're saying is, we start a new Latin American MSES? And implement the SIT program? Start putting dresses on those Don Juan, macho Latino men down there?

Yes Director Yanket! We did it before and we can do it again!

Applause… Applause… Applause… USA, USA, USA, USA…. (Clapping for Mary's response). Yeah! America First! Exceptionalism!

Several minutes later…

Geeeez… Mare, these guys sound like the Ku Klux Klan. (Jane whispers).

Yeah Jane, very Trumpish, Trampish, Dumpish…

Yes we can do the **SIT®** program, but with a new spin on it. This time we setup a new grading category for a lesser quality Whoring Stations. If we have a C grade for common, why not have a C1, C2 & C3 and so on. So we start a Latin American MSES® with grading system for the LA-MSES. For example, the C3 grade would be for the lowest quality. Where the SIT® Whore is behind a glory hole wall with only her-his **LCT®** [4.D-G2.27] penetration hole accessible.

Sure! We're with you on this, out of sight, out of mind, right? Works for me! Haaa ha… Don't ask, don't tell. As long as you don't let them immigrate up here and dilute the quality of the Pure American Whoring cum-munity.

Oh sure, same rules apply! Especially now President Donald aka the Douche-Bag Dump built the 20 meter high border wall with drone patrols. Haaa… haa… Despite most of it falling over.

Director Dune, it sounds very plausible to me. I'd have to discuss the plan with the rest of the cum-mittee and the President, because I don't wipe my ass without the president permission. But I think…. (Mary interrupts).

Well Senator **Gramma** (Lindsey Gramma is the Chair of the Senate Cum-mittee on Presidential Ball-Licking), what I told you wasn't the whole plan.

Oh! There's more? I have to perform a penis massage for the President scheduled for six-o-nine!

Oh yeah! I'll make this brief. And I don't want to make light of the **SIT®** program for, Sissies-in-Training. Like I said mine and my wife's Dads are products of the SIT program. But in Latin America we don't have enough effeminate type men to put a dent into how many Sissies we need for labor compensation, **LCT®**.

Well, well… What we're doing with the Contra **Vaganus®** Rebel groups down there is a swap deal, I'm I right? We give liberty to the young ladies who were gonna be put into prostitution servitude for rich families and we infiltrate their society with more free Vaganus®. Win! Win!

Wow! This is news to me.

Well it's a work in progress as an experimental project. This is conceivably what might happen. We bring the young Latino ladies here to the USA Inc. set them up in a breeding farm. Then the Latino Sissy Babies, the **LSB®** [4.D-G3.13] is shipped back south of the border. Creating an ad-Dick-ted, enslaved cum-munity which falls into a debt-peonage with America!

It's fantastic! Huh! Wow Dune. You're a real mover and shaker.

I try Sir. In the future if there are any Transitioned human Sissy-Boys we can eventually replaces them with the real Latin American Sissy, the **LAS®** [1.A2.7]. So basically the same thing we did here in the USA Inc.

Director Dune, Pardon me, this is a little off topic. I'm just curious about you and your wife's Dads, why are they still working as Common Whores?

Oh! My Dad is only working part-time because he's a grad student at Peniston University in New Jerky. And Jane's Dad is a real slut and loves being a Hoe, so the Whoring-Station® is his life. But they both only have one more year till retirement.

Hmmm… I see. But after retirement they'll be required to serve in the US Sissy Reserves, **USSR** [25.26.2]. They would need to snap into action when a Nation Sexual Emergency occurs?

Yes Sir. And like I was saying, their replacements are all original Breed-from-Birth BfB, pure Sissies. I think they're the only Transitioned Sissies, SIT Whores still works there. Here in the USA Inc. we're phasing out humans as Sissies. This is all part of the Anti-Gayness **Amendment** [17.29.1].

Well good for them! Don't forget the Sissy was breed out of the DNA of the super-friendly, non-violent, American Gay human **Sis-Gene®** [18.9]. And yes, Man-on-Man experimentation is still legal but it requires filling out the **MOM69** form.

Exactly! And yeah we're very proud of our human Sissy Dads.

Director, I have one more question.

Yes Director Yanket?

Well as you've stated, if the quality of the Latino human breeding women is questionable due to the lack of family **Cockage**® [2.B.0] records… (Mary interrupts him).

Dr. Yanket! Can I just say something about this?

Sure, sure, go on.

The Holy Cockolic Church has most of the records needed to formulate a partial record. The Church confiscated all the data when they bought the Catholic religion. But the problem is most of those records show a dominant Stud-Lineage in the Latino Cum-munity.

Wow! Okay, the Latinos are hung is what you're saying?

Yes Sir! Like horses! So like I was saying, we could start the breeding process with the Latino ladies and find out we're getting Sissy babies with really big penises!

Well Director, haaa haa ha… We're not breeding FEMs here! Not like we couldn't use more of those fine specimens of manhood in a dress!

Haaaa… Haaa… Haa… Haaaa… Haaaa… (The Cum-mitty room bursts open with laughter). Lady-Boys! Why not!

No problem, I'll fill out the **MOM69** [4.D-G5.6] form! (Yanket actually loves getting it on with crossdressers, which requires submitting the Man-on-Man sex permission form). Here, I got one in my back-pocket.

Right, right. And you know, this is why I suggested lowering the bar in the LA-MSES.

Director Dune, I just have a bad feeling about lowering the quality of the MSES to meet another cultures **Cock-Lineage®**. Hear me out. If in India they can castrate the balls off men and turn them into Eunuchs why can't we perform surgery on our well hang Latino Sissy livestock?

So what are you saying Dr. Yanket? Do the same procedure as we perform on the **Transmutation®** [2.B2.11] rejects here?

Yes! The **Mutts®**, when the Sissification procedure doesn't work we whack off their Dicks!

Whoa! Whoa! Whoa! Slow down! Don't you think this is a little harsh! And creepy! I'm not sure I buy into your suggestion on humanitarian grounds. (Mary is freaking out about it). I mean,

Jizz-Us ... !!!...

The madness has to stop! (Mary is waving her hands giving a cease and desist negative signal to the cum-mittee).

Oh, oh, oh… I'm sorry Ms. Dune. It was a figure of speech. We don't whack anything off. We do a penectomy on them. I mean, we leave about three centimeters so they can impregnate a Sissy breeder. After the surgery it's basically a big clit. But they're mutants and wouldn't exist if we didn't save them in the first place. So no foul play here.

Wow! I love how the USA Inc. Cunt-gress justifies making profit from the suffering of others. But, you have a point there Yanket. The **Transmutant®** folks were humans.

Right Dune! We saved them from dying in a FEMA [4.D-G7.13] camp. So the same procedure can be performed on the livestock we breed and own, it's the same. (Senator Cuming puts his two cents into the discussion).

Yes Senator **Cuming**. I don't see anything wrong with it, other than you have a creature that can't breed as easily because they're practically missing most of their cum-hose. But hey! Size, I would know being a DOM®, doesn't really matter. It's about sharing love the **Bonobo-Way®** [22.19].

Hmmm… Yeah Dune, size is an option. Haaa haa... I just thank the God-of-Cocks I'm a Stud! Well we're doing the humane thing here by not reducing the pecker length too much.

Right we're just doing a size reduction procedure, right?

Correct! Huh! (Mary heavily sighs from the cummittees ghoulish suggestions). And the new size will be about the size of my Assistant Jane Goldberg. Stand up Jane and show the Cum-mittee your precious little erect Sissy-Clity.

Wow! (They gasp as Jane lifts up her mini-skirt and proudly displays her erect clit to the Cum-mittee). Okay that looks really, really small! Geeeezy Weeeezy! It's a peanut!

Well Jane is a **B-Type®** [1.A2.2] so they're all pretty small (Jane without her Clit-Sock on ejaculates in the direction of the Cum-mittee).

Wow! She shoots really far! My gracious! What an aroused little temptress Gurl you got there Director Dune!

Yeah, I'm proud of my Gurl! And the Sissy babies would by MSES standards need to have a Penis Official Length Certificate, the **POLC®** [4.D-G1.3] of the appropriate length. It's strictly regulated here in the US-MSES, see Appendix A: Social Classes (Worker & Whore) Qualifications in the SM069 Manual. So I'm assuming the same standards would apply in Latin America as well, in the newly formed LA-MSES.

Okay, Ahh… Thank you Ms. Goldberg (Jane's still fingering her **Vaganus®** and squirting load after load in front of them). This sounds like a much better scheme providing the re-sizing is the correct length!

I'm sorry! Once I get started it's hard to stop. (Jane apologizes and sits back down next to Mary).

Yes Assistant Director Goldberg.

But wait a minute Dune. I'm not clear on something here, what category are we producing on the **Breeding Farm** [1.A2.6] Category 4 or Category 5?

Oh! This is a good question. The Farm is currently only breeding B-Types, so the category is 5. Category 5: Sissy-Clit®. Meaning, one inch or smaller in length in an aroused state.

Wow! Okay this is a revelation to me! So since when have we ever strictly only bred Bitches? I mean, it's a pair of Sissies. There's a DOM for each Bitch. And you know this Director Dune!

Yes, yes of course I know this! I'm a **DOM**® married to a **Bitch**®. Without my guidance my Bitch wife would be all over the place. As we've just observed by her unsolicited performance in front of us. There's a reason why Bitches have a collar and a leash on! And hey! What I just experienced overseas by trying to proliferate the world with ASB® is appalling! The **ASB** is nothing more than a lapdog! Just a sex-pet to the rest of the world. Sissies are being abused! There're is no DOM Gurls delivered with the ASB so the human females are going to be their new dominant partner-owner. Meaning the Sissies will be cum a sex slaves, beaten and caged like animals.

But the **POOP**® [4.D-G8.1] program was decreed by an Executive Order from the President to spread the domination of Sissydom® to all parts of the world! This negated all previous regulations governing what we can and cannot do.

You're right Senator McCuntell. Director Dune, the **IMF** [21.A.6] orgasmization is working to foster global monetary domination through cooperation, insecure financial instability to control the Whores-for-Profit markets. If you have you have any insecurity issues with getting the Vaganus product to market on time and under budget, then you're the problem!

Wow! Now I know why you're the President's favorite Ball-Licker! Listen! I've been given the daunting task of placing a

Vaganus® into every household and to also install the payment control devices, the PDE® on the entire population of the planet. Nobody has a bigger job than I do!

Chairperson, you of all people understands I had to take this one by the balls. If I step on a few testicles along the way, I'm sorry.

No, no, no... Mary, it's fine, it's just, I was not briefed on the rule modification for the POOP® program. You're doing a fine job. Keep me up! I mean keep it up. (Seymour interjects to referee the cum-mittee meeting).

Seymour its fine, we're going to be working very closely with the DHMC and the Sissy Trade Department, the STD. We can't do this without your cooperation!

[8.3] POOP

6 hours and 9 minutes of meeting later...

Well, all this discussion about penises has got my mind wondering. And this is slightly off topic but, my wife and I were on vacation. And it just happened to be near a FEMA Camp. So we went out for a bit to eat and we were surprised to see there was roasted Non-Stud (NS) Penis on the menu.

Ughhh! Senator that's GROSS...!!!... Okay, spare us the details!

Jane I'm gonna throw-up (Mary turns to Jane and says moving her fingers in and out of her mouth).

Yeah kind of gross, but with a little Sissy-Poop® sauce on it my wife loved it. And it smelled great!

Oooh! Wow! You mean, Disgusting...!!!...

Yeah well, she liked it! I didn't eat it of course. Stud class women order stuff like that, especially Girls like my wife. She's been divorced six times, engaged nine and has a real hatred for men in general. You know, it was like looking at sausages, little tiny mini NS sausages!

Well, it's definitely an all American specialty dish. (Senator Mitch McCuntell chimes in). My wife loves those FEMA camp little tiny roasted sausages. And hey! There's plenty of those poor bastards in the labor camps, what they gonna do with penis?

Oooh yeah! It was in both the American Gourmet and the USA Food Magazines. I think it was rated the best for Female gourmet dish of the year in 2253. I read a recipe NS man-sausage with a creamy cummy sauce and a dash of poop. It looked good! (Senator Lindsey Gramma proclaims).

Okay talk about being way, way, way off topic. I think this is the end of the inquisition of Director Dune. We're sorry it took so long.

No problem! My thanks to all the Cum-mitty members.

Thank you again Director Dune you're definitely blazing new trails for the creation of an American Sissydom globally.

[8.4] OFFICE

Back at the POOP office...

Wow! Somebody stop the world I'm getting dizzy. Shoo... I survived that gang of twisted psychotic demons.

You were great as usual, Mare. Where do you cum up with this stuff? Swapping prostitute for Sissies in Latin America?

Oooh Honey like most politicians, I pull it out of my ass!

Oh! Okay, well that explains everything. Haaa haa ha…

Talk about ass, cum here you! Ahhhh… Thanks for showing off your beautiful little body for me at the meeting today. Kiss… I love you. Mwah…

Anytime Boss! Love you too. Ummm…. Mwah…

Okay **Clitty**, Kissss… Mwah… (Mary gives a wet-kiss to her secretary and Clitty Cocque feels-up Mary). Ahhhh… That feels so good thanks Clitty. Mwah… You're a Sweetheart. I needed a good titty massage. Okay! I see the phone lights blinking, what we got?

Ms. Dune **Jamitin** is on line 6.

Okay Clitty, I'll take it. Jam-it-in!

Yes, my dear **Mary**, anytime you want me to. Haaa haa…

And you know I will let you *Jam-It-In* anytime you offer your beautiful African manhood to me! What do you have for me today besides teasing me about your Big Black Beauty my good friend? (Mary and Jamitin are on a video call and he's waving his erection in fully view). Ahhh… You tease! Give me some good news Dude!

Yes, great news, Mary!

Awesome what's happening on the Dark Continent?

Well the latest figures show the AU is now officially the only orgasmization outside of the USA Inc. which is generating revenue from implementing the American LCT® system.

It's fantastic **Jammie**! Let's celebrate! You and the African **CI®** worked so hard on the new African Union AU-MSES payment system. What platform did you finally use?

Mary **WeeeChat** of course! It's the only social media to use nowadays!

Right, WeeChat is in every Cuntree. So Jamitin, can I get you to talk with my other networks, the CI® in Russia, India and the Church affiliates on how you implemented the system?

Yes of course! For you Mary, I will do anything!

Great! I'm planning a Sissydom Conference which will be attended by 69 Cunt-tries and will have many attendees.

Where will it be held?

At my old school, my Alma Mater, the FUCIT.

Great! I'll be there and my wife Sarah and I will very much like to spend more intimate time with you and Jane again.

Yes Jamitin, our bed is your bed.

Okay we'll book the flights, just let us know the dates.

Jamitin, it will probably be on June the 9th. And I have some new ideas about the Middle-East Cunt-tries and your network in Africa. We'll have to talk more. Mwah…

Yes, please share your thoughts they will always be well cum. Thanks my good friend gotta go. See you soon Mary.

And you to Jamitin. Mwah...

Okay! Its message time, Clitty!

Yes Mam. Here's the run-down. President Dump, just six minutes ago, Turkish President, Iranian Prime Minister, Brazilian President, six US Senators, nine Russian Assembly Members, two Directors, a guy who sounded Muslin I think his name was Omar. He said he did the Hajji with your Bitch, an old high school teacher Mr. Cockum he said he wanted to re-penetrate with you. Then there were two guys who you and Jane showered with in freshmen year at FUCIT, Jane's Mom Sandy, then...

Put Sandy on the phone now! Okay Mam, she's on line nine.

Sandy! Is everything alright?

Wow! You sound just like a frantic father!

Haaa... Haaa... Yeah well I am the father of our child. What's up? How did the doctor visit go?

Had the sonogram today and everything is fine with our FEM Gurl.

Great! That's it, Sandy?

And guess what?

What? We're busy here at the office.

Her dick looks really big! Haaa… Heee… Haaa.

Of course! Hey gotta go! Love you. Mwah… Mwah…

Love you too Mary, tell Jane Hello, kiss her for me.

Okay, Kiss... Kiss… Bye, bye.

Put Dump the douche-bag on please. Yes. Mister President?

Ooooh Mary, hey I needed to go over the African stats and the Russian situation. And you know I'm partial to the Russian involvement in everything I do.

Sure, sure… We're having the breakthroughs we were expecting in Africa with the AU. They like the cash flow of the LCT® payment network. We'll achieve total penetration in several years. The Russians, I'm not sure about. But I feel if I sleep with enough of their politicians they'll relinquish control of the entire economy to Sissydom®. We gave them a taste of the Vaganus® now we wait for their total subrogation.

Great! So we're on track with the Russian. Pooty is my buddy. The Africans I really don't give a shhh…it about them. They called our Cuntree a shithole.

Yes President. But isn't your family, I mean the whole clan of you. Your ancestors, Trump, Tramp and Dump don't they account for why this Cuntree is a shithole?

Dune! I don't like you talking trash about my relatives! The Re-Pubic-Cunt party is the supreme Aristocracy. Let's just use more of the Non-Stud working class slaves I created with tariffs! No president ever created more disparity then me. I'm GOD! I don't know why the Africans hate me! I'm perfect!

Wow! Huh! (The President is so far off base from what they were talking about Mary doesn't know how to respond to this asshole). As we agreed, the formula of less weapons of lethal force mixed with an increase of Vaganus® works. Our enemies are be cuming our allies with the increase of Sissy pussy being propagated into their economies.

Wonderful, I'll tell the Joint Chiefs of Shafts to start putting dresses on the soldiers! We'll use Ass-Pussy Power! Haaa haa… haaa.

Yes Mister President, pink ones with crotchless panties! Heee heeee… Gotta go, nice talking to ya.

Thank you Marty.

Thank you Sir. My name is Mary, Mary Dune. Goodbye!

Wow! What a jerk-off! The Stupidest President ever in American history. Clitty, which Director sounded the most disparate?

The Breeding Farm Director Ma'am, he's been waiting six minutes nine seconds already.

Okay sure get him on the line.

Okay he's on line six.

Hello Director **Yu Jacket**. What can I do for you?

Hello Director Dune, I'm so glad to be speaking with you!

Yes, Director Jacket how's it going out there at the farm with Senator Humpme?

Ooooh he's a piece of work! And please call me **Yu**.

Sure, isn't Yu a Chinese name? Yes it is, my Mother is Chinese and my Dad is American.

Great! I'm so fascinated by the China culture and I would love to visit there in the near future.

Oooh well Director... (Mary interrupts).

Please Yu call me Mary.

Sure Mary, our family would love to have you visit them. Let me know when and I'll contact my brother-in-law who works for the Ministry of Animal Agriculture. Because Sissies are band from China nowadays. We'll need to get you in through secret channels.

Yeah it's a shame we can't open ties with our old trading partner just because of our sexual orientation.

Right, I mean who cares what hole you put it in!

Well **Yu**, it's a matter of what kind of hole. In this case the Americans prefer livestock animals to human hole. I think this has got everybody freaked out. But the Russians and Africans are kind of softening up to the idea.

Yeah well who knows what tomorrow may bring! Geopolitics is a mess game with President Donald Dump in cum-mand.

Right, but we have our first batch going up to Mars?

Yes, it was our first batch of one year olds to leave the Farm. I'm hoping they're going to be handled well on the voyage.

Ahhh… Yu, they're trying to convince me to take the first trip up with them.

You should go! It would be an adventure to visit the Red Planet.

Haa Haaa haa… Yu I don't have time for stuff like that. Hey you should go!

Haa Haaa haa… Please I'm a single guy, six hundred and ninety screaming one year old Sissy Bitches doesn't turn me on. Haa Haaa haa… Granted the Sissy matures faster than a human child does.

Yeah Yu, Bonobo Gurls are fluent at one years old and can climb a tree. But, you got a point there, they are a hand full, I have an adult Bitch as a wife and can't control her.

Right, it's an amazing genome. The typical Homo-Sis-Sapien Gurl can do calculus at five years old.

Yeah but Yu, I really wanna go to China and talk to the government officials about providing services to China for the bases on the Moon.

Cool! I'll set it up. You'd be going in on a visa for animal research. Highly restricted. Only Party members and scientists will be able allowed to penetrate you.

Excellent! My wife and I love a good probing!

Ooh! Mary, what I really called about was the Latin Sissy Babies the LSB® Clit length reduction.

Yu, how's that experiment going?

Great Mary, they were all reduced to category 5, Bitch length.

Cool Yu. Okay we're good on that then. So great, talk to you later, gotta go, see you soon.

Okay Mary, see you.

Who else we got Clitty?

Well Jane's been on line six with Popoff for sixty nine minutes, they seem really chummy.

Yeah, that's my Gurl! I told her to work her up into a freeze for her so we can strike a deal with the Russians! Next, who do we got?

There's the Vaticum insisting you report to Rome to assume the position as the *Mother-Superior*. Holy-Poop! Book the tickets! I can use a good Holy FO®.

Okay Next?

Uoooh! The **Contra-Vaganus** [20.1] leader **Juan Puta** (EN10) left a message.

Ooooh what does that prick want?

He wants to surrender!

Oooh! Another Holy-Poop moment! Jizz-Us! When it rains it pours! I can remember the last time I saw this guy. I broke a heel on my combat pumps tramping over a cobble stone street in Buenos Aires looking for his hid-out. When we finally found him he was already showing signs of being ad-Dick-ted.

How's that? (Clitty asks).

Well he immediately and incontrollable started dry humping me, like a crazy rabid dog! It was obvious he'd been sticking his dick in a Vaganus®. His rebel buddies probably didn't know he was getting some Sissy-Pussy on the side.

Well his message was, if Senora Dune puts out for him he would sign a peace treaty.

Okay, it sounds super erotic. Yeah! Book a flight to Argentina. I feel a road trip cuming on. But, this is the last one before the Holidays.

Who else Clitty?

Cardinal **Jackeroff** wanted to know if you wanted to reschedule your weekly Cumfession and Holy Cum-Union.

Ahhh… I don't have time this week, contact her back and schedule a quadruple Penance when Jane and I get back.

Next as far as political position, we had the President of Brazil left a personally message. He seemed very anxious to talk to you. It sounded like he had a business proposal.

Well try to get him on the line, its sounds like a perfect opportunity to develop a much needed Southern Hub of the LA-MSES.

Okay! Next there was the Senators, what do you want me to do with them, the standard reply? Fuck-Off!

Ahhh… Yeah, I mean it's the same thing every time, they want my ass, I want concessions, and it's always a business-fuck which often times goes nowhere! So yeah, standard, blow them off reply. I mean unless the message is like our Brazilian friend who sounded like they have a sweet deal. Wait! We'll send Jane to play with the Senators, just as a tease, I know they really want my ass!

Okay I'll setup an **FO®** with them and Jane in the rotunda of the Capitol Building.

Ahh… Clitty, you said you had calls from the Russian Assembly Deputies? Was it Vladimir Putitinov?

Yeah, yeah... I think his nickname is Pooty.

Yeah, Pooty, this is what the Douche-Bag in the Whitehouse calls him. Okay see if you can get Poooty, the Leader of the Upper House on the line.

Okay! Mary. (Clitty smiles looking up at Mary with an idolizing share).

The last time I was in bed with this guy he was talking about contracting the Cockolic Church or some Pseudo American orgasmization aka Cock-Illuminati to manage the pay system on Mars for miners working up there. Huh! It just dawned on them, men need something more than just good pay-check, they need PUSSY! Wow, what a revelation!

Okay Mary, he's on line nine.

Hey Deputy Putitinov.

Ahhh… My Mary! How are you my precious friend!

Great **Pooty**, so how's the Mars project going are you getting ready to ship my cute little Bitches up there?

Da, da… We're shipping them up! Tell me you decided to accompany your sweet little man pleasing darlings to Mars?

Ahhhh… Poooty dear. I'll get back to you on that, save me a seat! Maybe after the Holidays. We got Cock-Mas cuming up.

You mean X-Mas?

No! I meant Cock-Mas. The Cockolic religion renamed the Holiday.

Oh right, right… The HCC holiday.

But hey Pooty, I really wanted to pick your brains about Islam. I mean, you know a lot about the Middle-East you have many clients there.

Da, da… Sure ask away my sweet Mary.

Well how hard would it be to introduce Vaganus® to the Muslim part of the world? Would it be a cultural shock?

Oooh! Well I'm sorry to say, next to impossible my dear. Ahh… Sure we sell Sissy Bitches to the wealth Sheikh's but this is a culture which has subdued the female population forever. It would be absolutely forbidden to parade around the Middle-East like Jane does. And I must say, Jane your wife is really hot!

Right, right. My lovely nymph wife would not be allowed to be in public.

So the answer to your question is, yes and no. For example we sell a lot of Sissy ass to wealthy people because, like all human men in the world. The Vaganus® is the new ad-Dick-tion. Everyone knows once a man dips his wick into a Sissy Vaganus® he pretty much prefers the Sissy to the human pussy.

So Pooty is there a way to penetrate the Islam world.

Well Mary the Russian approach is to build the trust of the groups at the top, then it's a top down cascade. In your case, it's just a matter of ad-Dick-tion of the top of society. Then you can propagate into the culture from there.

Okay I see what you mean Pooty. Just like the American Fascist or now the Stud® aristocrats did in your Cuntree. First they gained control of the government and then the citizens fall prey to the Oligarchy promises. In your case the penis enlargement drugged bigger dicks win!

Yes Mary, just do like we do. Feed them the Vaganus® candy and then they will be eating out of your hands. Oooh! And hey! Do not worry about being harassed in the Middle-East. Just stick a hijab veil on your sexy American Sissies and Walla! Of course I'm assuming you have trained Sissy operatives ready to be deployed?

Well, yeah, yeah... Pooty of course we do! Actually we do have branches of the **NSA**, **FBI** and **CIA** for Sissies. So yeah, we have Sissies who are trained for fieldwork, including me. We're trained in subversion, seduction and secretions.

Ahh... Secretions? Da, da... You spray your Sissy pheromones.

Yes! It's usually in either, Jizzzies, piss or poop. But I had Special Sissy Forces training in the military. So I can induce my clit to squirt. Which means I have three ways to infect my prey.

Wow! Mary, you sound like a real bad-ass, very dominant. Ahhh… I like this in my women, girl or gurl. Strong!

Putitinov, I'm a DOM®, this is what we do. Poop is just one way I have of seducing human males. For example, I did a little pooping in your mouth at the party we had with Cardinal Popoff.

Yeah, yeah… I remember! What a wild party. And it was the only time I've ever been offered Sissy-Poop as a consumable item. But hey! I liked it. American Sissy poop is awesome! Maybe it would make a good Stroganoff dish!

Yes, my naive friend but what you didn't realize was you were being feed a full load of Sissy pheromones which I passed on to you from my Pimp. So if you ever wonder why you wake-up in the middle of the night, in a cold sweat, craving Vaganus®, or the need to bang a Sissy whore every day, think of my poop load which you so willingly swallowed. Sissies are the new heroine and the Homo-Sapien males are the junkies.

Well Mary, you're analogy is correct. The Sissy Vaganus® is the new vagina. This is why the Russian Assembly wants to work with you. We have the same vision of the future as you Americans. Money…!!!…

Control the masses through pleasure

Give them all the free Vaganus® they want. And as a result of the euphoria they work for super cheap and the Oligarchy makes more profit, simple!

Ahhh… Yeah, something like that. Just remember Putitinov, we don't have to kill each other over this anymore, right? Instead of a cold war, we can have a super-hot Sex-War.

Right! Right!

Peace through Vaganus®

So! When are you Americas going to share the Genome formula with us, so we can start making our own Russian Sissy Gurls?

Haa haaaa… Pooty darling, not going to happen.

What? You don't trust Russians? We are friends! You shared poop with me! We made love, drank Vodka!

Look Putitinov, we'll make the Sissies, you make the money. That's the deal!

Ahhh…. But we need sexy Russian Sissies, real authentic breed from birth, beautiful, **BfB**® beautiful Russian **Vaganus**®.

We're working on it Pooty! Our laboratories are experimenting with different race, color, ethnicities, sizes, sexual aggression. We're making Latino Vaganus® for Latin America with slight size modifications. We'll produce the Russian versions too.

Okay, well I will propose this to the Assembly for approval.

Ummm… Putitinov! When will you Put-It-In my Russian lover?

Mary! Cum to Russia and I will go to Mars with you! Ummm… Me and you! We're fuck-buddies!

Yes, it sounds like a plan Pooty.

Ahhh… I miss you Mary, cum to me, we'll make love in space!

Oooh Pooty! I need you in my Coochee! (Mary hangs up).

Wow this is one horny desperate bastard! Okay enough calls Clitty. Agh! I'm done!

[8.5] BEACHHEADS

Well Jane the **Penisagon** [25.6.b] has their beachhead in India, Africa and Latin America. The President and the **CI®** have their money-whoring world domination started. The HCC has their One Cock World Order, **OCWO** [9.B.1] in play.

Great! But Mare, what did WE get out of it?

Good question Jane. More like what did the world get out of it?

I really don't like the way the whole thing went down.

What do you mean Mare? The **POOP®** [4.D-G8.1] is a success!

Jane, it's not that. What I'm saying is most of the ASB® delivered to these Cunt-tries will be mistreated. They're just looked upon as pets. Sexually toys. And outside of the USA Inc. they have no rights. There's no Sissy Rights Act to protect them out there. They're gonna be treated like animals especially by the human females.

Mare last I checked, according to the humans we are animals! And you know Stud class women have hate issue for Sissies. They don't want use taking their man's Jizzies!

Yeah I know. But at least here in the USA Inc. we're animals treated with dignity and respect. Jane look, all I'm saying is, I get it. Our government is, as usual, going for world domination anyway it can get it. It has always been like this. Either by the barrel of a gun or financial control or both.

Huh! Personally Mare, I don't give-a-poop about the geopolitical bullshit the Whitehouse tries to pull-off. The Douche-bag-n-Chief is obviously profiting from destroying the working class in our Cuntree.

Same here Jane! But if this whole cockamamie Vaganus ad-dick-tion scheme stops wars from happening! What the hell! I'm in.

Me too Mare! Mwah… No more killing, no more bloodshed.

Right! *Pussies for Peace*, that's who we are! Or are we, *Vaganus® for Peace*. Hmmm….? Whatever!

Yeah Honey! Sissy-Sex® promotes the **Bonobo-Way** [22.19] and will bring peace to this crazy human dominated world Kiss… Kisss…

Mwah… Look the holidays are here. Let's just go home for Cock-Mas and enjoy our families. Mwah…

Mwah… Sounds good Baby!

Oh! Before we go home we might have to take a detour to Rome and meet with the Pope in Vaticum.

Yah! Yah! (Jane jumps up onto Mary). Mwah… Thanks!

Yep! It'll be my Cock-Mas gift to you. Kiss… Kiss… I love you so much Mary. Kisss. Mwah…

And me you Honey-Bunny. Mwah…

[8.5] BALTIMORE

Ummm… Ummm… Ummm… (Mary's phone vibrating).

Who's this? Huh! It's time for bed! Oooh! Poop! (Mary exclaims after noticing who is calling).

What? (Jane asks with concern).

It's the General. This can't be good at this hour. Huh! Unless he's trying to get laid! It's way too late for official military business. Jane! Take your hand out of my cooch. I gotta answer this.

Sure! After the success of the Jungle-Junk mission they promoted you to Lieutenant Colonel, so they think they can just make booty calls at all hours of the night.

Hello! This is Dune. (Mary answers her cell phone).

Lieutenant Colonel **Dune**, this General Boner. Sorry to call you so late, but you're being called up to report for duty at Fort Didher.

NOW! Geeezzz… General, what's the assignment?

Colonel Dune, I need you to lead a battalion of about 690 Sissy soldiers into Baltimore to put-down an insurgent uprising. They're a rag-tag bunch of anti-Cock radicals. We think it's the Vagina Alliance Christians, the VAC [20].

Wow! Than all the reports were true. The economic disparity is creating a rebellion. Impoverished Americans are rising up.

Yeah Dune, it looks that way. The VAC even published a **Manifesto** [20.9]. Its front page in the Washingcum Post newspaper.

Okay, we'll be there! Thank you.

Hey! And Dune. Bring that sexy little Whore of a wife with you!

Tsss… Yeah Boner! Jane goes where I go, there's no separating us. See you on base. Mwah… Mwah… (Mary sends a goodbye Sissy salute kiss to her superior office).

Continued in EN05, Chapter 1….

=== THE END ===

Review Request & Suggestion

Thanks for purchasing this book or bundle (four book set). Please leave a review on Google Books, Amazon or Audible. Also to help our readers or listeners, we strongly suggest downloading the Empty Nation manual **SM069** to assist with the complexity of the story from any one of the following.

Audible.com, free after purchase as a Product Summary

Amazon.com, (low price) ASIN: 1719912866

Google Play Books, (free) GGKEY: X02BGY24G4K

The Official Sissydom Manual SM069

The National Sissydom Association (NSA)
A subsidiary of USA Inc.
All rights reserved, copyright 2020
Revised: 02-09-2020

SM069-06 Description

The Sissydom manual version SM069-06 encompasses details from years 2213 to 2259. This manual is intended to be used by United States Inc. citizens for the sole purpose of clarification of the procedures, laws, rule, codes, regulations, probing, documents, exams, rating, ranking, classification, drugs, qualifications and behavior of all parties participating or remotely involved in the United States Inc. MSES (US-MSES).

TERRITORIES

This manual also applies to all occupied territories under control of the USA Inc. Including but not limited to all of Latin America (LA) including Cunt-tries in both Central & South America; refer to the LA-MSES.

SAR

Special Administrative Regions (SARs) enjoy a higher degree of autonomy under the "one Cock, one Cunt" concept developed by President Tramp. There are currently two SARs, Mexico located in the Central America and Canada in North America. Both were turned over to USA Inc. control after the NAFTA War in 2169. Both SARs mentioned here implement the LCT system.

Persons living in a SAR are NOT and never will be citizens of the USA Inc. Also neither is allowed to cross into the USA Inc. at any time (visas are not available) unless the border-crossing is for a female surrendering her rights and be cums a host-mother at a Sissy Farm Breeding facility.

MSES AFFILIATES

Although the following Cunt-Trees are not controlled territories or SARs of the USA Inc. they are dependent and liable to the USA Inc. monetarily. This pretty much means, the USA Inc. can squeeze their balls at any time to induce compliance.

IN-MSES (India)
RU-MSES (Russia)
IS-MSES (Islamic)
AU-MSES (Africa Union)
SE-MSES (Southeast Asia)

These Cunt-Trees are all implementing the MSES LCT system of payment (aka the new SWIFT system, see 23.27). For local rules and regulations consult the specific sections in this manual (section not available yet).

RULES

The rules and laws stated in this document are lawful and can be used in a court of law to defend and protect only the rights of United States of America Incorporated citizens. The USA Inc. governing body (Government) and any and all of its proxies or entities, owned, contained, endowed, funded, imprisoned, underwritten, confiscated, authorized, financed, detained, sanctioned, annexed, blockchained, begotten, empowered, captured, incorporated, forfeited, convicted, subjugated, forsaken, subsidized, sponsored, abandoned, franchised, promoted, controlled, conquered, incarcerated, entitled or restrained by said Government or its affiliated corporate members are fully relieved of any and all liability of wrong doing created by adhering to the laws, rules and regulations stated here in this SM069-06 document. Amen.

Please download the current manual for further details in Series...

About the Author

Empty Nation Series published by What Is It Press. As far as the author of the series is concerned, we know very little about the Sue Yan Nish. We think she is a Chinese-American and lives somewhere in China. And although her location changes frequently, we receive cryptic messages form her. The messages simply tell us only that the manuscript is finished and where we need to retrieve it from. We leave her compensation in a small box and in the same place the manuscript was left for us.

Authors Contact Info

The following addresses are ways to get in touch with the author Sue Yan Nish.

Author Bio:
https://www.amazon.com/Sue-Yan Nish/e/B07GW252V1

Emails:
sueyannish@outlook.com
sueyannish@gmail.com

Website:
https://sites.google.com/view/empty-nation/home